The
Arab
Way

Sherif Samaan

howto books

Please send for a free copy of the latest catalogue to:
How To Books, 3 Newtec Place, Magdalen Road, Oxford OX4 1RE United Kingdom
email: info@howtobooks.co.uk
http://www.howtobooks.co.uk

The Arab Way

How to work more effectively with Arab Cultures

Dr Jehad Al-Omari

howtobooks

Published by How To Books Ltd,
3 Newtec Place, Magdalen Road,
Oxford OX4 1RE. United Kingdom.
Tel: (01865) 793806. Fax: (01865) 248780
email: info@howtobooks.co.uk
http://www.howtobooks.co.uk

First published 2003

British Library Cataloguing in Publication Data.
A catalogue record for this book is available from the British Library.

Cover design by Baseline Arts Ltd, Oxford

Produced for How To Books by Deer Park Productions
Typeset and design by Baseline Arts Ltd, Oxford
Printed and bound in Great Britain

Contents

Preface

How do you define culture and who are the Arabs? Is it possible to exaggerate the role of culture, and can we generalise about the Arabs? Is it possible to write about your own culture and remain unbiased? Where do generalizations end and stereotypes begin in a work like this? Can a book of this type give the Arab culture some justice in the eyes of the Arabs themselves and in terms of its usefulness to non-Arabs? Where does this book fit in the overall global environment which every nation is supposedly undergoing? How does this book contribute to the overwhelming need for a better understanding of the Arab culture and Islam in view of recent events?

I believe that all the above questions are legitimate questions in assessing a book of this type. However, as important as these questions may be, they are not in themselves questions that this book pretends to answer. In writing this book, I had one objective in mind: to better inform Western expatriates and business-people who are relocating to the Arab World about some facets of the Arab culture which are of great relevance to them, in a simple, practical and concise manner.

In writing this book, it was inconceivable to ignore the bigger picture that underpins the choice of subjects and angles of discussion: namely the cross-cultural theory, its objectives, tools, limitations and failings. The book addresses the key issues that arise from my years of experience in the cross-cultural field and which every visitor needs to know either to eliminate uncertainty or to satisfy basic human curiosity. It is an attempt to help these visitors and sensitize them to common taboos and *faux pas*. At the same time, it would be pretentious to suggest that this book applies to every Arab you will meet irrespective of their age, sex, education and nationality.

In summary, this book aims to give guidelines and practical tips, to inform and raise questions, build bridges and demolish barriers, and finally, clarify a few misconceptions about the Arabs, their culture and attitudes. In writing this book I tried to combine theory with practice, to be user friendly without drifting into triviality. I have also made the assumption that my target audience is largely Western. I pray to the Almighty God that this modest book has succeeded in achieving what it set out to do.

Dr Jehad Al-Omari

About the Author

Dr Jehad Al-Omari is an experienced Cross-Cultural Management Consultant and has been training Western executives on Arab affairs and cross-cultural matters since 1986. A regular lecturer and speaker with international institutions such as Farnham Castle, Cranfield School of Management, the Netherlands  Institute of MBA Studies and Canning, he also holds a number of consultancy posts with numerous multinational firms operating in the Arab World. Dr Jehad Al-Omari currently divides his time between Europe and the Arab World where in addition to teaching on training programmes he supervises MBA students and is engaged in a number of expatriation and repatriation studies in the Middle East. For more resources and the latest information, you can visit the website www.a4arabia.com. He can also be contacted by e-mail at a4arabia@hotmail.com.

Testimonials

'Dr Al-Omari thinks deeply, is a wise man and a good teacher.' Richard Pooley, Canning International Training and Development

'Dr Al-Omari's seminars are world class. He has been one of the most professional consultants that we, as a company, have ever worked with (and our standards are very high).' Hans van der Linden, Managing Director, TMA Ltd

'Dr Al-Omari's seminars have broadened our view of the Arab world.' Nancy Helledie, Borealis A/S

'Dr Al-Omari balances the theory with practical application and real-life examples.' Garth GF Ward, Cranfield University

'Dr Al-Omari's teaching and communication skills are very high.' Sean Rickard, Cranfield University

Farnham Castle International Briefing & Conference Centre

A lack of cultural understanding and local practices can be a major obstacle to the effectiveness of conducting business in another country. The ability to relate quickly and effectively to colleagues and clients in a new country is very important to long term success.

Farnham Castle International Briefing and Conference Centre is widely acknowledged as the world's leading provider of intercultural management training and briefing and has an unmatched reputation for helping individuals, partners and their families to prepare to live and work effectively anywhere in the world.

Through its unrivalled faculty of trainers and experts, Farnham Castle offers a totally flexible and comprehensive range of programmes providing the first-hand knowledge and skills required to be successful in international business including -

◆ Workshops on developing Cross-cultural Awareness

◆ Working Effectively with specific cultures or nationalities

◆ Cross-cultural Communication, Presentation and Negotiation skills training

◆ Country and Business Briefings for any country in the world

◆ Intensive Tuition in any language

Full details available on web site at:
www.farnhamcastle.com

Acknowledgements

This book comes as a result of teaching cross-cultural issues for over 16 years throughout Europe, the Middle East and North America. During this time, I had the pleasure and honour to work with many professionals from whom I have learnt many aspects that have helped me in my chosen craft.

I would iike to extend my warmest thanks to Vincent Guy who was my first mentor and trainer and with whom I have had many useful discussions on aspects of the Arab culture and culture in general. I shall always be grateful to Mike Ward who has shown me many insights into the World of cross-cultural management and multinational teambuilding.

Thanks also to many individuals and institutions who have supported me in many ways and particularly to Jeff Toms from Farnham Castle, Richard Pooley from Canning and Garth Ward from Cranfield School of Management. I shall always be indebted to them and to Mark Trier from Language Solutions and to Hans van der Linden from Transnational Management Associates.

I am also very obliged to many friends and colleagues who have taught me much about life in the West, edited this book or previous work and given me many important comments. These are too many but I would particularly like to mention Dawn Attlesey, Peter Aylett, Julian Paxton, Anne Mills, Hayder Al Fekaiki, John Mattock, Steven Pritchard and Terence Brake. On many occasions, their interest in the Arab world and culture have given me many hints about what to write and from which angle.

Over the years, I have also worked for many organizations in so many different fields. I am grateful for their business and for their continued support. Without these organizations, I would not have had the opportunity or the audience to try and bridge gaps between East and West. Their continued support to international briefing programmes will make the difference to all those who aspire for true and everlasting multiculturalism to take roots in the new global economy.

Introduction

There are **three inherent difficulties** about writing this book in terms of subject, author and contents.

Firstly, culture is an infinitely complex, emotive, comprehensive and controversial subject. The role of culture, its impact and its presence in organizational life and at the inter-cultural level is open to many views and interpretations.

◆ What aspects of culture do you highlight or ignore and what is relevant and what is not?
◆ From which angle do you start your analysis and how far in depth do you need to go?

In this book, I shall take a many-sided approach to culture; using different methods, theories and sources, coming at the problem from a variety of angles. At the same time, this book will avoid long and complex analysis that is probably self gratifying but of no practical use to most visitors to the Arab region.

Secondly, there is something very personal and uneasy in writing about my own culture.

◆ How do I remain true to my culture without letting down the expectant reader?
◆ Can I achieve true objectivity without disregarding cultural sensitivities?

I shall try to give what I feel to be the safest approach or the least controversial opinion. This book is also one man's personal interpretation of his culture as viewed from several years, living in the West and training Westerners to work effectively with Arabs. It is also based on a deep understanding of prevailing Western attitudes to the Arab culture. I hope that the book will give its readers a framework and a starting point for exploring the Arab culture as well as addressing prevailing stereotypes.

Thirdly, we live in an age where everything is getting faster, and the average international manager is now handling several cultures simultaneously. They don't have the time to read numerous books about every culture they deal with, but rather they are in need of a concise, to the point, factual, definitive and prescriptive account of the culture they are working with. This book is a compromise between what the reader needs to know and my desire for some depth and sensitivity.

Notwithstanding the above difficulties, I hope that the book achieves its objectives of informing its readers and bridging a few cultural gaps.

WHO SHOULD READ THIS BOOK?

This book is a cross-cultural book first and foremost. By definition, this means that it is not a comprehensive, definitive or critical account of the Arab culture, but rather **a comparative and practical account** written with the Western reader in mind. It means that it focuses more on key differences rather than similarities, issues that Westerners will find puzzling, unusual or difficult to cope with. It is based on years of experience and a long list of frequently asked questions. It addresses Western perceptions and misconceptions of the Arab world, Arabs and Islam as well as some key Arab perceptions of the West.

The **target reader** could be the occasional business visitor and could also be the departing expatriate. Many practical tips are given on a variety of issues, from socializing to doing business. Some of these tips are common sense, and will apply to international travel, but others are specific to the Arab culture. Due consideration is given to Arab values and best practices, what I normally refer to as 'What makes Arabs tick.'

The readers will note that this book was written in a way that enables them to dip in and out after the first reading. They can come back and visit different parts of the book at various times and use it as a point of reference on specific issues ranging from hospitality to Islam and from desert outings to shopping. At the same time, it is hoped that this book will encourage its readers to seek out more information from other sources, be it the internet or other books.

Looking beyond this book, my advice to any reader with regards to working and living in the Arab world is very simple. If in doubt, ask colleagues and friends for help and find a mentor. Most Arabs, given half a chance, will be more than keen to help you out and to project to you an Arab perspective of their culture and their interpretation of world events.

Five Critical Questions

1. IS IT POSSIBLE TO GENERALIZE ABOUT THE ARABS AND THEIR CULTURE?

Firstly, it is inconceivable to envisage any scientific pursuit without the need to resort to assumptions and generalizations, and this is particularly true for social sciences. **In the cross-cultural world, we are often dealing with the art of probabilities rather than the science of certainties. Human behaviour is neither completely predictable nor utterly unpredictable but it is subject to norms, trends and patterns.**

Secondly, the Arab World, despite geographic spread and massive population has a lot of commonalties within it. To start with, there is the Arabic language, which is not only a means of communication, but also the prime media for exchanging information and the transfer of ideas and concepts, from Morocco to Oman. Then there is Islam, which is the main moral code that underpins the Arab way of life in every minute detail. There is also a common sense of history, which continues to present many Arabs with a golden age that influences not only their thought systems, but also their aspirations and how they see themselves and the world around them. Needless to say there are differences across the region, but it is has been my experience that these differences are no greater than those we find across the United States, Russia or even France and Britain.

Thirdly, this book does not pretend to give you the only truth or the whole truth about the Arab culture, but claims to be the first book written by an Arab to a Western audience with the aim of giving broad guidelines and practical tips from an Arab perspective.

Fourthly, this book addresses traditional Arab culture as a mindset and as manifested in collective behaviour not as interpreted at the personal level. You will no doubt meet many Arabs who due to their education and degree of Westernisation will not fit all the patterns outlined in this book, but they are the minority or the exception. The majority of the people you will meet will subscribe to many of the values and patterns of behaviour outlined in this book, whether they are related to attitudes towards time or style of communication.

2. IS THERE A DANGER OF STEREOTYPING?

There are two dangers that can undermine any book of this type - stereotyping and over simplification. Too many generalizations can mean that we potentially lock the Arab culture into a fixed stereotype, thus denying the Arab culture its sense of dynamism and ability to adapt to new conditions. Too many over-simplifications can easily mislead the reader into believing that the opinions and practical tips given in this book will simply apply to all Arabs irrespective of their age, sex, education, wealth, social background and so on. This would deny the essence of diversity that colours social existence the world over. The reader may ask, with justice, what about personality? Does it not affect behaviour and attitudes?

In this respect, this book comes with several cautions. Firstly, it is not intended to be a definitive account of Arab culture, but a simple-to-use set of guidelines and 'common sense' safe practices that may be of use to those who are not familiar with the Arab culture. Secondly, there are many situations where several solutions may exist, but the solution given was considered by me to be the safest or least controversial. Thirdly, we must always treat people as individuals not as cultural stereotypes, whilst recognizing that culture is largely responsible for shaping and polishing personality.

The interplay between personality, common sense and norms of behaviour is a complex issue that has received a lot of attention in cross-cultural literature. To start with, whilst personality can represent free choice in individualistic cultures, most cultures, no matter how individualistic they are, will set limits to the levels of freedom practised by the individual so as to prevent infringements on collective perceptions of what forms right and wrong, desirable or undesirable, efficient and inefficient and so on. Establishing what constitutes norms of behaviour is a simpler task in a collective culture where the individual has less room to manoeuvre in terms of expressing individual desires or exercising personal choices. Hence, we will always find patterns of behaviour that are imposed on the individual, irrespective of the individual's tendencies or wish to deviate, since society will not accept such deviations.

Finally, as much as culture does represent the sum total of human activity, endeavours, solutions and intellect, culture itself tends to shape and collectively colour much of people's behavioural patterns and mindsets in a subconscious way. It is thus not surprising that for most people, encountering another culture represents a turning point for them, as it puts them face to face not with the new culture alone, but with their own culture. Seeing ourselves as others see us is a major revelation for most people.

3. WHAT IS COMMON SENSE?

Common sense pertains when there are no clear written rules; it is a process that combines information gathering and interpretation to emerge with logical answers, conclusions or solutions. More often than not, culture consists of a set of unwritten values, beliefs and customs which are passed from one generation to another as the correct way to perceive, think and feel. Notwithstanding this, what is common sense in one culture maybe nonsensical in another, and vice versa.

To this extent, there are sometimes questions or problems where there are no clear rules or solutions, but which require a degree of rationalization to emerge with common sense answers. For example, what do you do if you are about to give a presentation to a group of Arabs, and how would that be different if the audience was actually American? This is where the **cross-cultural theory** comes to the rescue with its analytical tools, analogies and systems of derivation, interpretation and extrapolation. When these are applied to any one culture, we can emerge with reasonable, sensible, probable and likely scenarios and solutions that can form a set of guidelines.

The example of giving a presentation is very important here. We may begin by asking what are the ground rules with regards to the spoken word versus the written word? Are there any preferences or precedences to be taken into account? We may then explore the question of time and how it is perceived. Do people respect punctuality or is it secondary to other things such as mood, feel and type of event? Are there any natural breaks for lunch or tea or prayers? We can also investigate the rules and etiquette regarding hospitality and the guest–host relationship. Is lavish hospitality expected or is it frowned upon? Does it depend on hierarchy, and if so what is the role of hierarchy? All of these questions will lead to common sense answers and approximations about what *can* be done, what *should* be done and what *may not* be done.

Chapter 10 of this book approaches the question of doing business in the Arab World in terms of what makes sense and what does not. The fact of the matter is that there are no written rules about doing business in the Arab World, neither is there an Arab management theory. In this respect, the Arab culture as a whole serves as the foundation for exploring the subject of business. Another source was the cross-cultural theory itself in the shape of Chapter 3, which explores a number of key cross-cultural dimensions.

4. WHAT IS THIS CROSS-CULTURAL THEORY?

The cross-cultural theory has evolved in response to serious questions about the ever-increasing level and volume of international transactions and multicultural interactions. Multinationals have expressed serious concerns about the increasing cost of international failures and have shown interest in using culture as a source of competitive advantage. For example:

◆ What is the best way to manage the relocation of employees Worldwide?
◆ How do you train people to become effective international managers and how do you build a successful multicultural team?
◆ How is globalization influencing culture worldwide, and how do different cultures learn from one another?

Today, the cross-cultural theory manages to combine many disciplines ranging from anthropology to psychology, from organizational behaviour to leadership, and from communication skills to business ethics. The greatest achievement of the cross-cultural theory lies in its ability to produce neutral, non-judgmental, comparative terminology and literature that recognizes diversity as a source of richness, not conflict. Cross-cultural theory provides us with techniques and tools to study culture in a safe and non-controversial way, and with due sensitivity.

Over the years the cross-cultural theory has evolved and we are now at a stage when it is taught in most universities as part of the curriculum for students of management. Twenty years ago, it was barely mentioned or acknowledged. Today there are many cross-cultural models or frameworks that have been provided by pioneers such as Edward T. Hall, Geert Hofstede and Fons Trompenaars, and to the extent that we can now talk about 56 cross-cultural dimensions that have been observed. These range from face and guilt to mood and event, proximics and body language to directness and low context, and from leadership to hierarchy.

In this book, a number of these dimensions have been selected and explored in depth in Chapter 3 due to their particular relevance to the Arab culture. The importance of these dimensions lies in that they are non-judgemental, and so they do not suggest the superiority of one culture over the other but rather provide tools for making comparisons and emerging with practical conclusions. It is hoped that this book's exploration of these dimensions will be revealing not only of the Arab culture but also of the Western culture, thus providing the reader with some tools for self-contemplation and questioning.

5. CAN WE EXAGGERATE THE ROLE OF CULTURE?

Most cross-cultural writers and trainers are, by default, biased to the role and position of culture in international business. They would not be good at what they did if they did not feel a great deal of enthusiasm for the subject. At any rate, it is all too easy to exaggerate the role of culture on two scores.

Firstly, the reader must not think that culture will influence and dominate their international assignment in everything they do. Raising the subject of culture is not an invitation to try and find culture in everything you do, and more importantly, it is not a license to blame culture every time you hit a problem. To do either is nothing short of paranoia and my advice to the expatriate in this case is to take a break.

Secondly, readers should not find themselves preoccupied with knowing everything that needs to be known about Arabs and their culture. To suggest that is tantamount to stating that Arabs are not tolerant or hospitable to outsiders. Nothing could be further from the truth. The Arabs will make many allowances, and in many cases, they would consider it rude to point out to you that you have made a mistake.

Nonetheless, whilst we should not exaggerate the role of culture, we should not underestimate it or assume that it is irrelevant. In reality, many people tend to ignore culture until there is a problem. Culture must become a factor in considering business options, solutions, tactics and potential challenges. How will your counterpart react to bad news and how will you best approach a difficult subject? How can you anticipate possible reactions to a proposal and what can you do when competition gets fiercer? What is the best negotiation stance and how can you get the best out of a multicultural team?

All the above questions have many important cultural connotations. The importance of face and honour can never be underestimated when delivering bad news or working with hierarchical societies. Some societies relish and encourage fierce competition more than others. On the other hand, bargaining and long drawn-out negotiations are tolerated and expected in some cultures, whilst being avoided in others.

Delays in the decision-making processes and the importance of consensus management are more apparent in collective cultures than they are in individualistic cultures.

Ten Cross-Cultural Realities

PERCEPTIONS

In the next few minutes, recall your last visit to an Arab (or foreign country) – on business or vacation – and note down your experiences in terms of the following:

1. What did you enjoy most about this culture?

2. What did you enjoy least about this culture?

3. What annoyed or puzzled you most about this culture?

Keep these notes until the end of the book to see if these experiences have become more understandable, and particularly those that annoyed or puzzled you.

1. RECOGNIZING THE COMPLEXITY OF CULTURE

There are as many definitions of culture as there are writers on the subject, and probably more. However, all would agree on the complex, mercurial and emotive nature of culture. Culture is about values and beliefs, food and arts, costumes and customs. It is visible and invisible, it is trans-generational and ever-changing. The comprehensive nature of culture raises many complex questions about its meanings, applications and consequences. How culture manifests itself in negotiating may be different in its consequences for a retailer than for an industrialist, or a planner, or an engineer, or a sales-person or an architect.

Furthermore, cultural consequences exist at three levels. The first and most basic level is the **tactical level**: that is customs and etiquette, do's and don'ts, expectations and perceptions. These are relatively simple and straightforward in that they relate directly to culture, and they need few skills in terms of applying them to everyday use. At this level, it is the individual who is constantly required to flex his or her personal behaviour in order to get the best results, or at least in order not offend. Compromises are frequently made, contradictions are ironed out and simple solutions are found for complex problems.

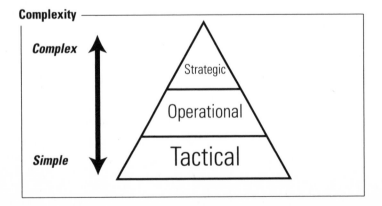

The next level up is the **operational or practical level**. How do people conduct business, what is a good manager, what are the rules pertaining to contracts, organization or leadership? At this level, the organization, through its management, needs to find new ways of implementing policies and applying procedures that are compatible with the culture. Cultural knowledge needs to be applied in a creative way to derive new processes that the organization can apply both internally and externally.

The final level is the **strategic level**, and this is about policy and change. How does culture affect different sectors of the economy from retailing to banking, and from service-oriented industries to manufacturing? What are the intrinsic opportunities or inherent risks in this culture? How do you introduce change, and at what level and what time frame should you plan for?

This book will focus on the first two levels, which are more practical and more in line with the needs of most readers.

2. GOING BEYOND VISIBLES

For many observers, culture can come across as being a fuzzy, vague, and sometimes trivial or even mercurial concept. It can mean many things to many people, and for some, it has no place in the real business world. On the other hand, culture is a personal, value -charged and emotive subject, which brings the need for a great deal of caution and sensitivity in the way it is approached. The dilemma is that it is too easy to trivialize culture by being too **touchy-feely**, and it is equally easy to dehumanize it by being obsessed with facts, bullet points and data, rather than meaning.

More Why's than What's

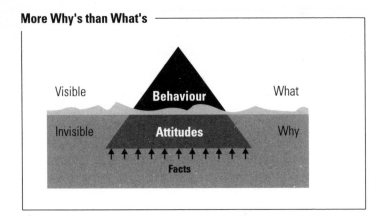

Culture needs to be understood in terms of what it means to its subscribers. What is sacrosanct in one culture may not be so in another, and what is a skilful job in one culture may be perceived as being normal in another. Our understanding and respect for other cultures must be based on respect for other people's values no matter how alien, strange or unreal they may appear to us. There are often deeper meanings than what we see on the surface.

When you are observing culture, you will come across many visibles such as food, dress, architecture and communication styles. These visibles resemble the tip of the iceberg, and they may or may not be truly representative of the real culture beneath the surface. You must never stop at **what** people do or **how** they behave, but **why**? What do these symbols, rituals and all that is visible mean at the deeper level: what drives them?

3. HOLDING YOUR JUDGEMENT

If and when you are confronted with an unusual, puzzling or disturbing situation or behaviour, you have to ask yourself one basic question:

◆ What am I seeing?

As in the diagram shown below, it would be entirely wrong to immediately blame it on the person, and personalize the differences or conflict, so to speak. It would be equally wrong to generalize what you see about the whole culture, and so emerge with stereotypes. How people behave, react and make decisions is extremely complex, and the role of culture should not be overestimated.

Human Behaviour

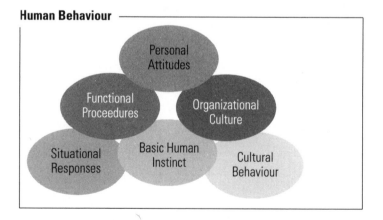

Personal
Attitudes

Functional
Proceedures

Organizational
Culture

Situational
Responses

Basic Human
Instinct

Cultural
Behaviour

Also remember that what you say about others says more about you than them. Your judgement as to whether someone is efficient or lazy, competent or useless, focussed or disorganized has more to do with your own cultural values than theirs. What may be an important skill, attribute or function of a manager in one culture may not be so important in another, and vice versa.

A good example is rote learning. In some cultures, such as the Arab and Chinese cultures, rote learning is an integral part of the educational system, whereas it is has become redundant in many Western cultures. In the Arab World, the ability to recite poetry and the need for leaders to be good orators remains strong, whereas it has lost its appeal in many Western cultures. In business this is translated into people's ability to rely on memory as opposed to memos and minutes. It also manifests itself in people's tendency to tell stories and anecdotes rather than constructing complex arguments.

4. APPRECIATING GANDHI'S DILEMMA

Let my house not be walled on four sides, let the windows be open, let all the cultures blow in, …. but let no culture blow me off my feet. Mahatma Gandhi

Culture has a direct impact on you personally, as an individual, as it relates to your values, ethics, beliefs, practices and many things you hold dear, worthy of defending or holding-on to, and have an emotional link with.

When you operate outside your own culture, you will not only come face to face with the other culture, but with your own. Your own cultural values and deeply held views will rise to the surface, and an inevitable discourse between the two cultures will emerge. How you deal with this discourse, rather than its outcome, and how you manage this process will form an integral part of **culture shock**.

To my mind, Gandhi's words summarize the cross-cultural dilemma eloquently and accurately.

◆ How do I become more international without loosing a sense of my identity?
◆ What is important to me and what is less important, or negotiable?
◆ What can I learn from other cultures, and what added value do I bring to this culture?

Only you can answer these questions.

In addressing the above questions, you will find that the easiest option is to crawl back into your own culture, limit your acquaintances to fellow nationals or expatriates and gradually fall into the expatriate ghetto or bubble. Try to resist that, and resist the 'them and us' mentality that characterizes many expatriates' mentality the world over. It is, of course, an easy option as you do not have to answer any of the preceding questions.

The alternative is to allow yourself to undergo some life-changing experiences that will inevitably widen your horizon, enrich your life and broaden your perspective. Luckily, it is has been my experience and observation that more people are choosing to go international for that purpose. In a recent study conducted on behalf of a Scandinavian firm, I found that the majority of expatriates accepted relocation as it offered them the chance to travel and experience different cultures and lifestyles. Salary was chosen as the third most important reason to relocate, whilst promotion was chosen as the least important reason.

5. ACCEPTING CULTURE SHOCK

Culture shock is the most normal reaction any person can undergo when moving from one environment to another. In a recent study I found that some 64% of the sample studied had undergone culture shock even though no effort was spared in preparing these expatriates in terms of relocation help, logistical assistance, cross-cultural training and pre-visits to the country.

Most people when being told that they are going overseas will undergo a period of apprehension, anticipation and excitement simultaneously. The prospect of promotion, a new job, a new house, free education for the children and the first few weeks as an honorary guest in a foreign country is what is often referred to as the honeymoon period. Once the exciting period is over, certain realities begin to hit home. Missing family, friends and routine is by far the most important reality. Not being able to speak the language and having to deal with different sets of rules is a major hurdle for many. Being uncertain about new friends and one's effectiveness and position is another barrier.

However, it is important to remember that you are not alone in this stage. Everybody undergoes this period of doubt, and for every nagging question you have, there are several people around you who are willing and able to help. All that you have to do is ask. Most people recover from this period of uncertainty after a few months at the most. They will begin to make certain surface adjustments, acquire new hobbies and habits, and settle amongst a new circle of friends. However, do remember that after a prolonged and happy period overseas, most people will suffer from a reverse culture shock when they return home. So be prepared.

It is further argued that when expatriates remain overseas well beyond the traditional two to three years expatriation period, they undergo a second culture shock, which is more far reaching than the first. The experience induces a more profound change in their personality, attitudes and perspective on both their own culture and the host culture. This is sometimes referred to as going native where the expatriate begins to enjoy staying away and dreads going home. This can be bad news on two fronts. Firstly, the expatriate will find it harder to adjust when he or she eventually returns home and secondly, they will find it even more difficult to adjust back into their company. The key lesson here is that expatriates need to maintain strong contact with home bases, irrespective of their expatriation periods.

6. KNOWING YOURSELF

It is useful to know something about other nations' habits in order to judge our own in healthier fashion.

René Descartes

If there is one recurring philosophical theme amongst all cross-cultural writers and trainers, it is that they all agree on the importance of knowing yourself, your culture and your key values. This famous dictum – know thyself – was inscribed on the temple of Apollo at Delphi in Greece. Socrates affirmed it, believing that only through self-knowledge could one find true happiness. Plato went even further. He linked an understanding of oneself with an understanding of the world and how it is ordered.

In the cross-cultural world, the need to know yourself takes a different set of priorities. It is about what you stand for and what you bring into the bargain. Your key values and added value. What are your negotiables and what are your non-negotiables? How do you perceive others, and why do you perceive them that way?

Self knowledge is about establishing dialogue between ourselves and our values as if we are viewing our values for the first time. When we enter into this dialogue, we will see our values in a different light since some of them will lose their magic grip on us or lose their emotional hold, and only then are we able to free ourselves from their restraint. We can begin by asking why we do things in a certain way and why do we feel certain emotions about certain aspects of our lives. Are these feelings normal or justified or have we been simply programmed to feel this way?

If and when we are able to understand why our cultures have evolved, in the way they have we will find it easier to understand how other cultures have also evolved and why they do not cherish or despise the same things we do. In other words we will respect difference and accept that our way is not necessarily the only way, and every now and then we may admit that their way makes more sense than our way, at least in their environment. Self contemplation is a necessary tool in this process but good old and long drawn-out discussions with colleagues from other cultures are highly recommended on this score.

7. SEEING YOURSELF AS OTHERS SEE YOU

If only we could be given the power to see ourselves as others see us, it would free us from many a blunder and foolish notion. (Paraphrased)   Robert Burns

There is no doubt that seeing ourselves in the eyes of other cultures can bring out the best in us by enabling us to put our culture in perspective, neither perfect, nor inadequate, and neither superior to others, nor inferior. It moderates our views of the world and of ourselves, and enables us to be who we want to be rather than what we were brought up to be.

Travelling and working internationally gives us a sense of maturity, which would otherwise be denied to us if we remain at home. There is a definite link between knowing ourselves and seeing ourselves as others see us. The more we become aware of how others see us, the more we get to know ourselves, and the more we are able to free ourselves from habit and embrace choice. Indeed, the world of today is changing very fast, and we have to learn to change with it and not be left with habits and methods that do not belong to the present world we live in.

Interestingly, whenever I have raised the subject of seeing ourselves as others see us with Western trainees, the reaction has always been astounding. To start with, there is a basic human curiosity to know more. It is an exercise that most Western expatriates are happy to embrace, unlike other exercises I can think of. However, what has always struck me as being unreal is the tendency of most Westerners to think that the world sees them in the most negative way. They will always emerge with responses such as 'colonial', 'arrogant', 'promiscuous', 'immoral', 'greedy' and so on.

It has always been my job to try and explain as well as moderate the above answers. The responses are themselves a good reflection of the Western mindset, which is essentially self-critical. This is both good and bad. Whilst self-criticism is good for character, too much of it can be demoralising. I try, therefore, to encourage people to think of more positive things that outsiders see in them, such as their 'efficiency', 'honesty', 'punctuality' and so on. As the next section will try and demonstrate, expatriates need to be aware about how they are stereotyped by others as a starting point for making entry into this culture or the other.

8. WORKING WITH STEREOTYPES

In the real world, perceptions and stereotypes are common, and most of us have them. These perceptions are a form of generalization, and they could be right or wrong, positive or negative, realistic or exaggerated. However, perceptions can become stereotypes and they become fixed, non-negotiable and, therefore dangerous. Stereotypes are irrational and unfair as they have a tendency to compare our best ideals with someone else's worst realities.

Nevertheless, it has been observed that international managers who admit to having stereotypes are on the whole more likely to perform better than those who deny having them. Being able to reveal and confront one's own stereotypes is the first step to banishing them altogether.

However, how you are perceived by other cultures is a different matter altogether. Do remember that perception is reality. It really does not matter whether these perceptions are true or not, but what matters is how you will deal with them and what you are going to do about them. Think of them as strengths and weaknesses. Capitalize on the strengths and try to address the weaknesses. Begin with the following questions:

1. What is it they admire most about my culture?
2. What is it they admire least about my culture?
3. What should I do more of as a consequence?
4. What should I do less of as a consequence?

If you ever have a chance to ask a colleague or a group of colleagues from another culture any or all the above questions openly and without inhibitions you will be amazed with the quality of discussion that will follow. You can also pursue the above questions on a corporate to corporate level.

I recall once training a multinational team of Indian and several European nationalities on a team building exercise. We asked a small group of Indians and English managers to go away for an hour and a half and come back with a presentation on the Indian culture. The Indian managers were supposed to brief their English colleagues about their culture. About twenty minutes into the exercise the Indian managers declared that they could not go on with the exercise as their English colleagues were unwilling to reveal their perceptions of the Indian culture out of politeness. The impasse was resolved when the English managers agreed to give these stereotypes in writing and their Indian colleagues started addressing them one by one. At the end of the appointed time, the English managers were able to give a very good presentation on the Indian culture.

9. MENTORING AND SOLVING PROBLEMS

Most cross-cultural research suggests that international managers will benefit considerably from finding local mentors they can refer to every time they hit an uncertain or sticky situation. The local mentor is someone you can trust to ask the embarrassing or simple questions without fear of showing ignorance, and it is the person you can refer to when you need an explanation for one thing or another.

The key dilemma that faces every international manager is how to cope with uncertainty. How do you handle differences, how do you prepare for this task or the other, how do you interpret a client's response? And there is always the 'What If' scenario. Mentoring and being able to have a reliable and credible point(s) of reference is the key to success in the international arena.

At one point or another every international manager will come to the realization that they don't know many of the answers to the questions that this new environment throws at them, and that they can't do it all on their own. They have to move from an attitude of independence to one of interdependence, from suspecting the 'locals' to trusting them, and from ethnocentrism to polycentrism. Ethnocentrism means that *our way is the best way* or *there is no other way*. Polycentrism stipulates that *there are several ways* and *our way may or may not be the best way*.

Polycentrism further stipulates an excellent approach to problem-solving along the following lines:

1. What is their way of addressing this problem or challenge?
2. What is our way of addressing this problem or challenge?
3. What can we learn from their culture?
4. What can they learn from our culture?

In addressing the above questions and in the sequence specified you can be sure to achieve two objectives:

1. Ensuring that your foreign colleagues or counterparts are not inhibited from giving their opinions since you have allowed them to state their position first.
2. Ensuring that cultural difference results in a learning experience rather than creating an atmosphere of cultural imperialism where head office rules dominate. You are well on your way to becoming **glocal** thus combining *global vision* with *local imperatives*.

10. PACKING YOUR SENSE OF WONDER AND HUMOUR

It has always been my experience that when you are living overseas, the first two things you should pack are your sense of wonder and sense of humour. It is said that curiosity and open-mindedness are two of the most important requirements for a successful international career. It is impossible to envisage where we would be without curiosity. True and everlasting learning starts with curiosity.

◆ Why do they do things in this way, how do I react, how do I gain their trust, what can I learn from them, what do I bring to this culture or where is my added value as far as my hosts are concerned?

These and many other questions are what spurs the successful expatriate to integrate and be part of what is going on, rather than being a passive, and a negative observer.

At some stage, we have to be able to laugh at our own mistakes, brush them aside and put them down to one of life's many experiences. To see ourselves as others see us requires a good sense of humour and the ability to put things into perspective. They are not wrong, they are just different, so are we. Observed from a distance, some of our values do not make sense to people from other cultures, and things that can make perfect sense in one culture are sometimes farcical in another.

My first dinner party in the UK was a nightmare for both myself and my hosts. I broke all the rules pertaining to good etiquette in the UK including arriving late, not emptying my plate and kicking up a fuss when I was told I could not smoke in the house. In addition, I thought that my hosts were rude and believed that they were trying to get rid of me as soon as I walked in. The reality was far more complex than that, and I was able to laugh at this first experience with my host some years later.

Today I also realise that the way we used to entertain Westerners in our Arab home was farcical or a bit of a nightmare to many of them and to us. We could never understand why they always insisted on bringing presents with them, write to us immediately after the event or eat everything that we put in front of them.

I hope that by the end of this book, the reader will appreciate both the apparent and subtle differences that exist between the Arab culture and the Western cultures as a whole.

The Arab Culture in a Generic Context

WRITING ABOUT CULTURE

Interestingly, whilst the Arab world continues to receive a lot of attention from writers on history, politics and religion, this degree of attention has not been matched by cross-cultural writers. The importance of this section and this book in general is that this is the first book written by an Arab that takes the cross-cultural angle or argument as the starting point in explaining the Arab culture to a Western audience.

There are now many widely available 'generic' books about culture, and there are also a number of established writers who have written 'reference books' on the subject. Most prominent amongst these writers are Edward T. Hall, Geert Hofstede, Fons Trompenaars and Nancy Adler. Their work was pioneering, original and had far reaching impact on the subject of culture and its credibility in the academic and business worlds. They have explored and unearthed many dimensions of culture ranging from attitudes to the social environment, time, regulations, power, communications, risk and so on.

This book is influenced by the above writers although none of them have ever written specifically about the Arab culture. This section tries to capture some of the key learning points and lessons from the cross-cultural, generic and comparative study of culture. It would have been a shame not to have done so. I have consistently tried to expand many of their generic concepts in a practical hands-on sense, and tried to bring their work into reality both in the generic and Arab senses.

The generic perspective explored in this chapter is designed to provide the readers with a comparative tool to their own cultures and other cultures that might be familiar to them. Some reference will be made to the American culture or the Chinese or Japanese cultures to add contrast which will hopefully make things clearer in the minds of the readers. This chapter will also include many practical tips which are well established in the cross-cultural theory. Most of them will be particularly relevant to the Arab culture, but many of them will also be relevant to other cultures such as the Chinese, Indian, Latin American and some African cultures.

THE FOUR CULTURAL DETERMINANTS

With reference to the works of the Gurus referred to earlier, there are four determinants that underpin the Arab culture, and these determinants have been observed elsewhere whether in China, Africa or Latin America.

Firstly and most importantly, the Arabs are simply **high collectivists** as opposed to being individualist. In a nutshell, collectivists will put their family, tribe or country ahead of themselves, and for them values such as honour, face and hospitality are critical. In fact, it would be possible to generalise that 60% of Arab values, attitudes and behavioural patterns derive from deeply held collectivist values and beliefs.

Secondly, the Arab culture demonstrates all the key features of **high power distance** cultures where bureaucracies are plagued with numerous layers and power brokers and where exclusive privileges and perks are expected for those at the top.

Thirdly, the Arabs are definitely **high context** cultures where collectivism and the need to save face is helped by complex and sophisticated communication systems which are on the whole more implicit than explicit.

Fourthly, the Arab culture is considered as being **polychronic** on the whole which is characterized by the complex management of time where several tasks are managed simultaneously and where timing and diplomacy can override the need for urgency.

Cultural Determinants

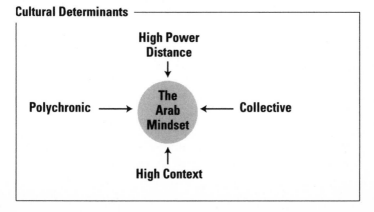

More about these determinants and their impact on business practices in the following pages.

RELATIONSHIPS IN COLLECTIVE CULTURES

Collectivism is one of Geert Hofstede's five dimensions of culture. Collectivism prevails when people are integrated into strong, cohesive groups, and where the interests, opinions and decisions of the group or the whole are considered to be superior to those of the individual. The opposite of collectivism is **Individualism**, which pertains when relationships between individuals are not strong, and where individual choice and freedom is often considered to be superior to collective choices .

If we start with mainland China then we come across the concept of **Guanxi** (network) where loyalty to this network is very critical to succeed in business or government. With Japan, collectivism takes a **national** dimension where family loyalty comes after loyalty to the nation but where **me** is not as important as it is in the case in the USA where the order starts with **Me and My Career** then **My family** and then **Everything Else**.

Collective cultures are driven more by relationships rather than task, shame rather than guilt, and harmony rather than facts. To the Japanese, **politeness** is almost a religion, to the Chinese **humility** is a sign of power, and to the Arabs, **hospitality** is about integrity and honour. Collectivism also manifests itself in terms of reliance on **networks** to do business and the use of **intermediaries** in resolving conflicts. In collective culture, the emphasis is placed on **consensus** and **consultation** in the decision making process whilst open conflict is avoided where possible. In individual cultures, the rights of the individual are paramount and consensus is replaced with open debate and confrontation avoidance is replaced with combative negotiations.

In collective cultures, the importance of relationships can never be underestimated. Success in business and in many walks of public life is highly dependent on the individual's connections, whether these connections are inherited (tribal or family position) or acquired through hard work. Collectivist cultures are thus non-egalitarian in their approach where position and status can dictate a mode of conduct that varies according to the individual being addressed.

Collective cultures can be patriarchal cultures such as the Arab culture, but they can also be matriarchal cultures such as the Indian culture and many cultures in the South East Asia. In both cases, old people are highly revered and age is respected. The concept of old people's homes which is common in most individualist cultures is abhorrent, to say the least, in most collective cultures. The diagram below shows some of the key characteristics of collective cultures.

Collective Cultures

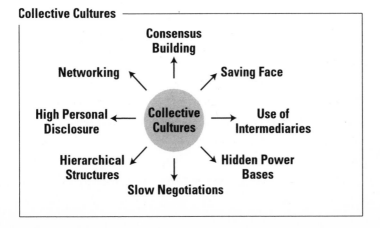

BUSINESS PRACTICES IN COLLECTIVE CULTURES

1. **Small talk** is not a waste of time, irrelevant or an intrusion on privacy. Most collective cultures find it important to establish trust and warmth before the business is done. It is a ritual that precedes every meeting, and pleasantries are genuinely appreciated and reciprocated. Small talk can also act as a diversion tactic particularly when either party feels that a confrontation is eminent. Small talk thus provides an opportunity for both parties to review their positions before negotiations resume. If you happen to come from an individualistic culture, you may find that some of the questions appear to be too personal from your perspective. The advice is that you should persevere and be diplomatic.

2. **Personal:** Be sure that it is you the person they are doing business with, and not an abstract entity (your company). Getting to know you is an integral part of the process, and vice versa. It is your word that they will trust, and it is you that they will blame if things go wrong. Take your time in building and cultivating personal relationships. In difficult situations, making personal pleas and the use of emotional arguments are common. As embarrassing as it may feel to you, this is not emotional blackmail. In most individualistic cultures, it is the custom to de-personalise business to make it easier, especially in difficult or tricky situations. The advice in collective cultures is that you should make work problems your own problems in order to win help and sympathy.

3. **Disclosure:** Most collective cultures tend to be hot on personal disclosure. This openness represents a bonding ritual that may conflict with the famous English Reserve. Personal disclosure takes many forms including private questions regarding background, family, financial status and the exchange of anecdotes or personal stories. When people disclose personal information they expect you to reciprocate.

4. **Face:** Collective cultures are sensitive about loosing face. Communications are implicit, intermediaries are used and negotiations are lengthy. Don't cause anybody to loose face but be prepared to show steel. The bottom line here is 'hard on issues, soft on people'. Most collective cultures find it difficult to say 'No' directly and bluntly so they will use phrases such as 'it is difficult' or 'leave it with me' or simply 'maybe'. They are not being evasive for the sake of it, but trying to save your face as well as theirs. If you want a straight answer, it is up to you to request it, repeatedly but politely.

5. **Decisions:** You may not get to meet the real decision-maker until late in the negotiation process, so allow for this. Give your counterpart enough time to refer matters to decision-makers, don't give many concessions prematurely, and give yourself room to manoeuvre when you meet the decision-maker. In most collective cultures, consensus and long consultation periods are typical, so be patient. Power bases can also be hidden and there may be several power brokers in any one organization. You need to do your homework to establish who makes the decisions and allow yourself time before decisions are reached.

6. **Intermediaries:** When things are going well intermediaries are expensive, but in sticky situations, they are worth their weight in gold. Networking and using intermediaries is often the best way to resolve conflicts and for putting indirect pressure on your counterpart. These intermediaries can be commercial agents, representatives or colleagues, but beware of false friends. Some people will promise you the earth but they are unable to deliver. Check your intermediaries' capabilities and simply don't rely on their word for it.

7. **Networks:** Collectivists rely heavily on the use of networks to establish credibility or for the purposes of conflict resolution. By lining up potential intermediaries or people who can bring pressure to bear on your counterpart, you are well placed to resolve most conflicts early enough rather than allow them to fester. In cases of conflict, asking a friend to mediate is sometimes the only way of re-starting dialogue. You can increase your chances of success through personal referrals rather than making cold calls.

8. **Conflicts:** Open conflicts are mostly avoided in favour of surface harmony and in order to save face. Surface harmony means that communication is always kept at a diplomatic level and that you are relying on implicit rather than explicit messages. However, if something is outrageously ludicrous, don't hesitate to express this openly and explicitly. Open conflicts can be a way of putting pressure on you, but beware of good actors who will put on a fuss just to force another concession from you.

9. **Contracts:** Contracts and written agreements are necessary tools but it is people who implement them. Goodwill, trust and mutual respect are worth more than what is written down, which is often negotiable should circumstances change. For our friends we interpret the law, and for our enemies we apply the law. In most collective cultures, it is your word or that of the decision-maker which will drive the contract, rather than the contract driving both parties. When either or both parties start referring to the contract, it is a sign that the relationship was never there or that it has failed and it is time to re-establish the relationship through face-to-face dialogue.

10. **Continuity:** Changing key personnel is disruptive and dangerous. Ensure some form of continuity since you are relying on goodwill not contracts, reputation not agreements. If somebody is good at what they do keep him or her, on the job, if not, pull them out quickly. Remember that in collective cultures business is personal. The dilemma here is that most international companies do not have the mechanism that enables them to convince key staff to remain overseas for long periods of time.

11. **Consensus:** Although decision-making is centralized in most collective cultures in that it rests with the head of organization, the need to build consensus remains essential. This means that the process of building consensus through various means of influencing tactics takes a long time as opposed to democratic votes. It also means that some decisions can take a long time especially if they are controversial or touch on the interests of several groups.

12.Evolution: It is in the nature of most collective cultures that change happens by evolution rather than revolution and so it takes a long time to initiate and implement change. The need for consensus building, surface harmony and the prevalence of hidden power bases all contribute to the length of time it takes for change to happen. Collective cultures are traditional cultures which respect tradition and resist sudden change, especially if it is imposed.

HIERARCHY IN POWER DISTANT CULTURES

Power distance is the extent to which members of society within a country expect and accept that power is distributed unequally and that differences do exist according to status. A typical **high power distance** organization is prone to a high degree of centralization and where structures are essentially tall or multi-layered. Within high power distance organizations great wage differentials tend to be the norm, and senior managers come to expect many status symbols. Management styles tend to be paternalistic and less democratic than low power distance organizations.

In the ideal world and the world of Islam and tribalism the Arab world should manifest all the traits of a low power distance culture, but in reality this is far from the truth, especially at organizational and official levels. Indeed, whilst Islamic teachings preach egalitarianism in many different places, and whilst the essence of tribalism lies in equality, it seems that the Ottoman hierarchical systems of government that dominated Arab life for several centuries have left a permanent mark on

Arab society. Against this, there is a real dichotomy between the real world and existing practices and the traditional ways of Islam and tribalism. Indeed, we can state that this is in an area where a big gap exists between Arab-Islamic heritage and values and the real world, and this gap is felt most when we are looking at organizational structures both in the private and public sectors. Furthermore, when we begin to observe society at large and how it is evolving, it is very noticeable that a class system is gradually emerging throughout the region and very much in spite of islamic teachings and tribal values. Needless to say that the extent to which high power distance attitudes prevail in the Arab world varies from one country to another and from one organization to another. It is most felt in countries such as Egypt, and least felt in rural areas and smaller family-owned organizations.

High Power Distance Cultures

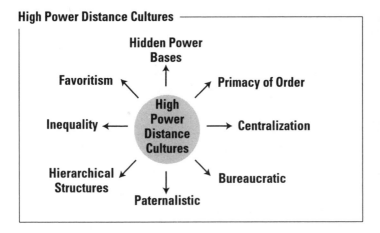

Hence it is possible to suggest that whilst the Arab organization tends towards **high power distance**, the society at large continues to operate in a more **low power distant** way. The following business tips relate to the organization not the society.

BUSINESS PRACTICES IN HIGH POWER DISTANT ORGANIZATIONS

1. Bureaucracy is the name of the game for most high power distance organizations where red tape, complex systems and procedures prevail. Within most organizations, bureaucracy results in rigidity where individuals are highly bound by the rules and they will show reluctance to take initiative, that is if they are empowered in the first place. Individuals become adept in sticking to their job specifications and their position as the basis for not doing anything.

2. High power distance organizations are by definition tall and hierarchical organizations as opposed to flat organizations. The organization could consist of numerous layers and sub-layers that in themselves create bureaucracy, rigidity and lack of transparency. Access to decision-makers becomes very difficult in these organizations and the process of decision-making becomes complex when the agreement of several parts of the organization becomes essential.

3. Decision-makers are frequently hidden from outsiders or sometimes not so obvious to determine on the basis of organization charts. These decision-makers may seek to hide behind subordinates, advisors and assistants to the point that it is difficult to reach them. As difficult as this may be, always seek to identify who the decision-makers are, and try to reach them if it is at all possible.

4. There is an inherent lack of transparency that is confusing to the outsider, and opens the door to rumours,

speculations and misunderstandings. This lack of transparency emerges as a result of complicated rules and procedures which can come across as being impossible to implement and even contradictory. This lack of transparency opens the door wide open to accusations of favouritism and sometimes corruption.

5. Organizations tend to thrive on the need for order and discipline within the organization, and to the extent that there is a regimented attitude to position and lines of authority. Some large organizations will have volumes of procedures and rules that specify everything to the individual – from the smallest task to simple common sense steps. The only way to cut through this red tape is through personal contact and networks rather than trying to follow procedures correctly. In these organizations, personal contact can make the most complex of issues simple, and the lack of it can make the simplest of tasks a nightmare.

6. In negotiations, do not expect that the real decision-makers will be present every time, and do not confuse their lack of presence as a sign of delegation. Decision-makers will frequently use intermediaries to save themselves from any potentially embarrassing moments during the negotiations. Clearly, the sooner you get to meet the decision-maker, the more quickly you will achieve your goals or at least reach a decision. However, in negotiations do not give all your concessions until you meet the decision-maker, as he or she will demand some concessions as a sign of authority and shrewdness.

7. Do not assume that delegation and empowerment to employees is going to be widely accepted. There is often a degree of apathy towards empowerment since it involves responsibility, which in turn involves liability. This is certainly true for collective cultures where there is a tendency to dilute decision-making on the basis of collective responsibility rather than individual initiative and enterprise. Typically, the lack of empowerment produces an atmosphere of low morale amongst employees who will always claim helplessness in front of the more powerful members of the organization.

8. Technical or advisory committees are bad news all way round. If you are making an offer and it is referred to a committee there is a strong possibility that your offer is not sufficiently convincing, which in turn justifies diluting it with the technical committee. Committees are sometimes employed to delay decisions or to justify unpopular decisions. Committees are also sometimes employed to deflect accusations of favouritism and corruption by pretending to take away the decision from hidden power brokers and bases.

9. Dress-code, name-plates, titles, personal-stamps, car parking space, certificates on the wall and the size of the office are some of the key trappings and symbols of power in the typical high power distance organization. Don't shrug them off as superficialities but try to read them and interpret them correctly.

10. Hierarchy in terms of who meets whom and who is seen to be making the final decision or signing the contract is

all too important. Bypassing correct procedures and going beyond one's level may be regarded as a challenge to the individuals involved, and may be taken personally.

COMMUNICATING WITH HIGH CONTEXT CULTURES

The American writer Edward T. Hall first coined the terms High Context and Low Context many years ago. They relate largely to communication styles across cultures. Today, High/Low Context is a well-recognized model that has many interpretations beyond Hall's initial definitions. Most research that has been done on Hall's work in this field has been of a qualitative rather than quantitative nature and there is not a lot of statistics on that score, not that it matters in the context of this book.

The Arab culture is on the whole classified as **High Context** culture along with the Chinese, Japanese and to a lesser extent the British. High context cultures are essentially cultures where their systems of communication are so complex and diversified that they rely heavily on body language or non-verbal signs, intonations, idioms, euphemism, anecdotes and hidden meanings to the extent that the spoken word is simply one of several means of communication. Low context cultures such as the Germans, North Americans, Scandinavians and to a lesser extent the French tend to emphasize much more the spoken word where the general rule is say what you mean.

In difficult situations, high context cultures tend to relay the meaning implicitly or below the surface, whilst low context cultures are more likely to be explicit. Whilst high context cultures are driven by relationships (collective), low context cultures tend to be more individualistic and are as such more task oriented.

Furthermore, whilst a high context culture may appear to the North American as being evasive, vague or slow, a low context culture may appear to the Arab as being impersonal, impatient and rude. Hence indirectness in high context cultures is no more than a form of politeness that is easily misinterpreted as being evasive. This is particularly relevant when bad news (rejection or termination of contract) is involved where the deliverer is careful not to hurt the feelings of the recipient of such news, cause them to loose face or at least to minimize the shock effect.

Nevertheless it has often been observed that when two high context cultures communicate, there can be four times the confusion given that the subtle hints of one culture may go missing on the person from the other culture and vice versa. To this extent, the most relevant advice in international communication is to continuously check that meanings and concepts are understood through reviews and repetition. People are advised to employ several communication tools ranging from writing before meetings to writing after meetings. In this respect, it has been observed that in cross-cultural meetings, the **circular agenda** can be more effective than the **linear agenda**. More about agendas later on in this book.

High context cultures are also characterized as being descriptive as opposed to prescriptive. In prescriptive cultures we note that there are always clear guidelines and rules that prescribe individual behaviour in a multiplicity of circumstances. In other words, norms of behaviour in prescriptive cultures are predictable as the rules are clear to everyone involved. In descriptive cultures, the rules are unclear and the individual is sometimes unclear about what to do, and so it is left to their initiative and enterprise.

Prescriptive cultures are on the whole uneasy in situations of uncertainty and thus they require as much certainty as possible in terms of what and what not to do. Most Western cultures in this respect are uneasy when the rules are unclear or when they do not know what is next. In prescriptive cultures, living with uncertainty is part of everyday life.

How different cultures deal with uncertainty does affect their ability to take risks, or not, as the case may be. In prescriptive cultures where every effort is taken to remove uncertainty, the individual's ability to take risk is enhanced, be it a calculated risk. On the other hand, in descriptive cultures, the individual's ability to take a calculated risk is severely limited and thus risks are leaps of faith or a form of blind faith.

High Context Matrix

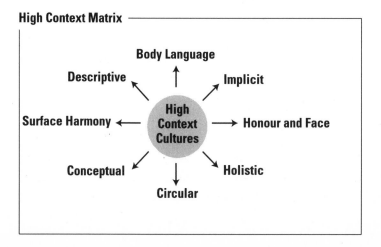

COMMUNICATING ACROSS CULTURES

In cross-cultural terms it is often said: 'How do I know what I have said until I know what you have heard'. In other words, when we are speaking across cultural or linguistic barriers, certain meanings can get lost, some words can get misinterpreted and subtle signs or hints are easily missed out. Accordingly, there are a number of key communication tips that one can follow, irrespective of the culture you are working with.

1. Don't get wrapped up in what you say but concentrate on what is being understood. Ask many open questions to elicit what has been understood and don't be too shy to return to the same point a few times. Address each issue from as many angles as you can and always seek to assess degree of understanding on the other side.

2. Be prepared to repeat yourself and to visit the same point several times. However, if you have not been understood avoid using the same words or phrases again - try different ones. Being misunderstood can cause more frustration than disagreeing with someone. Try to use diagrams or drawings, photos or videos where appropriate and it is always a good idea to try and summarize with examples of how things have happened or should be done.

3. Use short sentences and avoid long, conditional sentences or complex structures. Try to be as direct as the opposite culture will allow you to be. The clearer and more direct you can be, the less likely you are going to be misunderstood. However, do remember that being direct is not a license to be blunt.

4. Get used to 'offshore English', which is more universally understood than 'English English'. Grade your language, use simple words not sophisticated English, and avoid long sentences. Also avoid colloquial words, technical jargon or abbreviations unless you are sure that these are generally understood by your counterpart, even then watch for signs of lack of understanding.

5. Give examples and relate to case histories or memorable personal incidents rather than using generalizations. Learn to tell stories as well as listen to them. Remember that good stories are a lot more memorable than long drawn-out lines of argument. Also remember that the Chinese symbol for listening includes the heart, the eyes and ears simultaneously.

6. Rather than invest too much time in one long meeting, try to arrange for several short meetings. This way, you can control the information exchange to an optimum level, and it will allow you to take stock on what has been understood in the previous meeting.

7. It is a good idea to make the first meeting a general meeting whilst the second meeting is where the real business gets discussed in great detail. This way you can also ensure that your counterpart has a chance to refer matters to other colleagues if needs be for further consultation and instructions.

8. Remember that there are many cultures where people will be reluctant to admit that they did not understand what you have said. It involves loss of face, so do watch out for

the body language and for bluffing signals. Never ask people if they understand you as it can be very patronizing. It is your job to assess whether they understand or not.

9. Avoid the use of idioms or euphemisms unless you are willing to take the time to explain them.

10. Use several communication tools such as reports, fact sheets, models, diagrams, charts, photos and anecdotes to maximize understanding. But always remember that the spoken word is the most respected form of communication. Make sure that you contact people verbally before you write to them and do follow up written communication with verbal discussions by using the telephone for example.

11. Beware of false friends where certain English words can mean different things in other languages. Certain words have different connotations in different cultures. For example, the word problem has very negative connotations in Japanese and you are better off using the word difficulty or challenge. Equally, the word maybe can be yes in some cultures and it can be as good as a no in other cultures.

12. Allow for language breaks where your counterpart is able to break into his or her own language, particularly when the going gets tough. Do not be disturbed by this. Do remember that if your counterpart is speaking your language it takes a greater degree of concentration on his or her part.

All of this takes time and requires patience. Be prepared to spend more time than you have anticipated.

BUSINESS TIPS FOR HIGH CONTEXT CULTURES

1. Most **collective** cultures are also **high context** cultures in terms of communication and meeting styles. To start with, one has to listen carefully to every hint and anecdote. Watching the body language is also important whether it relates to personal space, eye contact, and the length of the handshake or the seating arrangements. Remember that in high context cultures, **if the body language conflicts with the spoken words, it is better to believe the body language.**

2. As far as **meeting styles** are concerned, high context cultures tend to be holistic in their approach to problem-solving. There is a preference to adopt what can only be termed as the iterative approach as opposed to the eliminative or linear approach in terms of managing issues. This involves several rounds of discussions as well as a degree of repetition to ensure full understanding.

3. Negotiation is a long, circular, repetitive, holistic and **iterative** process that requires patience and perseverance. Your counterpart will be testing your limits constantly. Allow plenty of time, be prepared to conduct the negotiation over several meetings and be prepared to re-open issues that you thought had been covered in previous meetings. Nothing is final until the contract is signed and sealed, and even then, negotiations can be re-opened should circumstances change. Being able to show flexibility and openness in these circumstances is a sign of integrity.

4. Everything is negotiable and expect all kinds of **tactics** from deliberate delays to tendering and re-tendering, and from unreasonable offers to using the competition to put pressure on you. Do come prepared with all kinds of scenarios. Spontaneous decisions or ideas are common but don't be surprised if they are retracted just as spontaneously. Lack of information or misinformation is an issue that faces every international negotiator, so whatever you do, make sure that your counterpart is not your only source of information. Within your team, make sure that you are all singing from the same sheet as your collectivist counterparts will be. If this is difficult, appoint a spokesperson.

5. Collectivist and high context cultures are good negotiators because they are **patient and persistent**, and they will try and wear you down. They will spend a long time probing your weaknesses and your limits, but don't take that personally. Don't confuse friendliness, which is genuine, with business tactics.

MANAGING TIME IN POLYCHRONIC CULTURES

According to international cross-cultural studies, Arabs are often classified as being **Polychronic** as opposed to **Monochronic**. Starting with monochronic cultures (Germany or USA), these cultures are essentially clock-driven where the key characteristics include doing one thing at a time, concentrate on the job in hand and sticking to plans religiously, and where people are often task oriented and where relationships are mainly functional. In these cultures time overrides relationships and task overrides personal feelings, in other words, business is business.

Polychronic cultures, such as the Arab or Chinese cultures, are relationship driven, and in many cases traditions of hospitality and common courtesy can be time-consuming. This is not the same as not respecting time or giving it any value. Furthermore, polychronic cultures are essentially multi-taskers in the sense that doing many things at a time is what comes naturally to them, and as a result, they are able to tolerate interruptions, digressions and are essentially holistic rather than reductionist. It is important to say that polychronism is not always associated with collectivism as is the case for the Italians, Spanish and to a lesser extent the French. The reverse is true for the Japanese, who although they are collectivists are also monochronics.

The cross-cultural theory of today as applied to international management skills, goes a long way to suggesting that there is value at either end of the spectrum (polychronic vs monochronic). There is no good or bad way, and there is no right or wrong style but rather that the function and circumstances should decide the appropriateness of the approach. There are circumstances when being polychronic is essential during brain storming sessions or where creativity is essential. There are times when being monochronic is the only way of getting things done.

Polychronic cultures are sometimes referred to as **event-driven** cultures, as opposed to **clock-driven**. In the former, it is **timing** rather than **time** that is the important issue. The outcome of a meeting is determined more by the circumstances and context that underpins it, rather than by a pre-determined agenda. The following tips attempt to highlight some of the key points and issues that are common in most polychronic cultures whether they are Indian, Arab or Chinese. They relate to a mindset that has a completely different approach to doing business from most Western cultures. Bedsides the Arabs and the Chinese, many Latin American and African cultures are also classified as being polychronic and within Western Europe some people would add the Spanish, Portuguese and the Italian as polychronics.

Polychronic Cultures

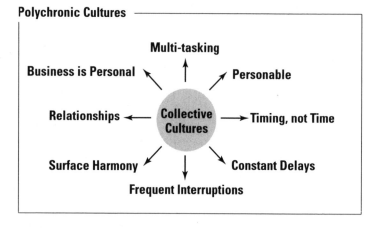

BUSINESS TIPS FOR WORKING WITH POLYCHRONIC CULTURES

1. Don't confuse **polychronism** with lack of **punctuality** or respect for time, they are two different things. In polychronic cultures, punctuality may be respected, but timing or the need to find the perfect time for raising a difficult issue means that not everything is subjected to the clock but to feelings, emotions and circumstances.

2. In **event driven cultures**, a good meeting where everything is going well may take much longer than originally planned. The attitude here is about 'capturing the moment' and making the best out of this opportunity. When the meeting is not going well, it may be terminated earlier than expected under one pretext or another.

3. The most important characteristic of polychronic cultures is **multi-tasking** or the tendency to do several things simultaneously. In the real world, this manifests itself in frequent interruption from sub-ordinates, colleagues, visitors and naturally the telephone. At the most extreme level, several meetings can go on simultaneously.

4. Consequently, it always pays to **allow for delays**. The worst thing you can do is to lose patience, as this will reflect badly on your personal attitudes and your image. Always give yourself plenty of time, otherwise you may end up leaving the country without getting an agreement, or worse still, you will give too many concessions just to get things done before you move to the next country.

5. Remember that your **time restrictions** could be used against you in a negotiating environment. Whilst punctuality and good time-management are perceived well, they could restrict your flexibility. If you are very clock-driven, you may come across as being rigid, impersonal and impatient. The art of crossing cultures is about managing the contradictions between conflicting values and attitudes.

6. Whilst there is an increasing awareness of the importance of time worldwide, polychronic cultures tend to emphasize the importance of **harmony** as being equally important. In China, building context must precede the bottom line, and in the Arab world hospitality is a must. In all of these cultures, surface harmony and mutual respect are prerequisites for good business. Trying to hit the bottom line very early in the meeting may be misinterpreted as being rude or discourteous.

7. Attitudes to time in terms of the **future** vary considerably amongst polychronic cultures but when it relates to the **past**, we begin to see some similarities. Most polychronic cultures are relationship-driven and past-oriented cultures, tending to place much emphasis on tradition, etiquette and history, and change is resisted. This reflects itself in the importance of continuity whether it relates to expatriation periods, hand-over periods or to aspects such as age and experience.

8. **Expect interruptions** frequently during meetings. The worst thing you can do is to take these interruptions personally or assume that they show a lack of respect or lack of interest. However, be warned that these interruptions can easily cause you to lose focus.

9. Always plan for **several meetings** rather than putting all your eggs in one basket. If everything gets done on the first meeting, then it is a bonus, and you can go back home earlier than expected. It is better to explain to your head office why you need longer time prior to departing on your mission than trying to negotiate it over the telephone.

10. To sum up, in polychronic cultures personal interaction is an integral part of the business environment. As well as personal questions, pleasantries and small talk you will be expected to socialize with business colleagues, exchange favours, advise on personal problems and so on. To this extent, **business is personal**. This also manifests itself in the prevalent use of personal or emotional arguments and in a business context, the manager is seen as a father figure.

The Business Pyramid

INCREASED COMPLEXITY

The preceding chapter looked at the Arab culture and culture in general from four different angles. The key characteristics of collective cultures were outlined in as far as they are relationship driven which has many implications. Some of these implications overlap with the fact that the Arab culture is also a high context culture and to a lesser extent the fact that the Arab culture is a high power distance culture. There is some overlap between the fact that the Arab culture is high context with some of the features associated with polychronic cultures.

To this extent, the aim of this chapter is to bring the findings of all the previous sections under one heading in a consistent and organised fashion. The diagram on the next page shows how doing business across cultures does get more complex in accordance with the task being performed. Communication is the first point of contact whether in person or in writing, and the skills associated with communicating whilst important are certainly less complex than managing meetings. In managing meetings, people have to go beyond communication to things such as etiquette, hospitality, order of things and agendas, whether they are written or assumed. Managing meetings is in turn less complex than negotiating or doing business as a whole since the latter incorporates a lot more issues beyond communicating and managing meetings. The summary that follows attempts to put some order into what has been discussed so far.

The Business Pyramid

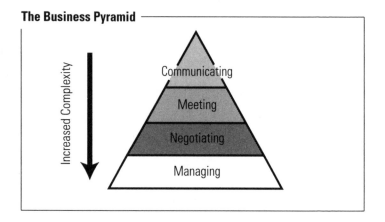

BUILDING A COMMUNICATION STRATEGY

1. **Saving face** is important in showing respect or deference to power. Diplomatic language and the ability to phrase criticism or objections in a subtle way are important to maintain relationships. Don't cause anyone to lose face, and don't allow others to make you lose face. Be prepared to use it to put pressure on or to draw the line. It is also a good negotiating tactic.

2. It is your duty to make sure that what you say is **being understood by others**. No one will admit to not understanding you for fear of embarrassment. Watch out for bluffing signs such as constant nods, it may mean that you are talking too fast or using too technical language, and don't bluff yourself either. It is bad communication.

3. Confrontation avoidance is about using the right language and not fudging the issue. Hard on issues, soft on people means that you should strike a balance between not causing others to lose face or get hurt whilst at the same time trying your best to stick to your position.

4. Watch out for hidden meanings, messages or even threats. Vagueness is not necessarily a sign of weakness, but sometimes a way of not hurting you. Watch out especially for phrases like it is difficult, I will do my best, leave it with me and even maybe.

5. Listen carefully to idioms and anecdotes, the answer will be buried inside the story and learn to tell stories yourself. Don't switch off when people embark on yet another story.

6. Watch out for body language and learn to be more tactile. If the body language conflicts with the spoken word, then believe the body language. Sometimes, where you are greeted and where you are seated is significant. Learn to interpret all of that correctly, and try to reciprocate. The same goes for how long it takes to offer you a drink or where your host says farewell.

7. The style is always likely to be elaborate and flowing. More often it is not what you say but how you put it across. Take your time, and don't rush. There is an emphasis on pleasantries and small talk to the point that similar greetings are repeated several times. It is a sign of warmth and a way of making you feel comfortable.

8. Remember that what you say is not important, but what the others hear is what counts. Always check understanding by asking lots of questions and repeating yourself if necessary. If you are unsure of your counterpart's standard of English try to cover the same points from as many angles as possible.

9. Take care of presentation and try to exceed expectations, but don't lose sight of substance. Your dress code is a lot more important than you may think, but don't be hasty on judging other people on their dress code or use of English.

10. Expect interruptions and learn to override them and take them as being normal especially with people you know well or in times of conflict. If you wait for your turn, you may never get it, and if you stop every time you are interrupted, you may never finish an argument.

11. When you are meeting senior officials, expect a lecture (spiel) at the beginning of almost every meeting. It is power distance at its best or worst. Don't take to heart everything that is being said. There is a great deal of difference between theory and practice.

12. Train yourself to listen to tone and tempo as they can carry more meaning than the words themselves. The same goes for gestures and use of space and eye contact.

13. Grade your English and supplement the spoken communication with written formats and sketches. At any rate, avoid giving out too much written material during the meeting, as this will take away from verbal dialogue.

14. The spoken word is superior to the written, and must precede it as well as supplement it. (Meet, Write, Meet - Phone, Fax, Phone). If you start communication with a written format, there can be an assumption that you are deliberately being formal, trying to score a point, or that there is something wrong.

15. What may be agreed in spoken words may not be written in a letter or contract. Few would be prepared to risk a putting a concession to you in writing as they may be held to question by superiors.

16. Remember that in many cultures, the prevalent business ethic is that my word is my bond, and what you shake hands on is what goes, rather than what you sign. What you sign will only be used in times of conflict.

17. Accept repetition and circularity as a means of ensuring understanding, and hence allow a longer time frame than is normal within your own culture. Circularity is also a great technique for changing the subject when the going gets tough, and it is also allows an opportunity for the opposition to rethink their position.

18. 'What is truth if it destroys harmony?' is a famous Japanese saying that summarises many business practices. Learn to restrain yourself from being too direct, and to minimize open conflict. Also learn to pace your argument over time in order to save people face.

19. Don't confuse high context and confrontation avoidance for lack of aggressiveness. It is about tact and respect. If people don't like you or respect you, they are more than capable of being direct.

20. Written communication is likely to be less it is common than in the West for two reasons. Firstly, the emphasis is always on the spoken word, and secondly, language fluency may be an important barrier.

21. The written language has a tendency to be long and flowery, especially with the older generation. Nonetheless, short and to the point written communication is equally common where language fluency is limited.

22. Where the written communication is long and flowery expect the bottom line to be hidden in the middle, not at the beginning or towards the end. Both the opening and closing paragraphs will be dedicated to pleasantries.

23. Faxes are frequently used, and to a large extent, they have replaced posted letters. However, it is very rare that people will treat faxes with any sense of urgency. If you send someone a fax, make sure that you follow it with a phone call.

24. Electronic mail is becoming more frequent, but the usual pitfalls on brevity and directness apply. As in the case of faxes, that sense of urgency may not be reciprocated.

25. Don't assume that if you write to people they will write back, they may telephone, and in some cases, they may expect you to telephone to supplement the written communication.

MANAGING MEETINGS EFFECTIVELY

1. Making appointments is always a good idea, and it is expected. However, do not make them too far in advance, and expect most meetings to be arranged at short notice. More often than not, people will expect you to make firm appointments a few days prior to your arrival, and that is normally for the first meeting.

2. Try to avoid open or brainstorming meetings where people are expected to be fully interactive, uninhibited or perhaps critical of each others ideas. The chances that people will not participate or others will get offended are exceptionally high.

3. It is not unusual for people to drop in, without appointment, for a chat or for business, and in certain cases, this level of spontaneity carries with it the element of surprise. You are under no obligation to leave when sudden visitors arrive, but generally take your cue from your host. Learn to join in the conversation and get to know these guests as they might be important for you in the future.

4. As a Westerner, you are always expected to be punctual, and punctuality is perceived as one of your strengths (Unique Selling Points). Whatever you do as a Westerner, don't be late and you will score a point in your favour. However, don't expect others to play by the same rules if they are visiting you or meeting you somewhere.

5. When you visit people and you are asked to wait, a degree of patience is important and this is normal. However, as a rule of thumb, don't wait too long, otherwise you may be sending the wrong message (you are desperate). Making you wait could also be a tactic that your counterpart is using to weaken your resolve or test your willingness to negotiate.

6. Notwithstanding the previous point, and as an exception, when you are meeting very senior people, expect a long wait before you are able to see them. Frequent cancellations, late meetings and sometimes very short meetings are common. Be prepared for all eventualities in terms of time flexibility and readiness. Also expect meetings with senior officials to be short so you have to learn to be extra concise and to the point in your delivery. Meeting these senior people could also be a formality before you meet the real business drivers or summing up before a decision is made.

7. When you visit people in their offices, do not be surprised to see other visitors, and they may linger on long after you have arrived. Your host may also start talking business in their presence. It is not an ideal situation but it is normal.

8. The general rules of hospitality dictate that a host has very limited ability to terminate a meeting in a direct way. Hidden signals and the general winding down of the conversation is the furthest people will go in terminating a meeting, but there are always exceptions with people who are exceptionally busy or highly Westernised.

9. Don't be surprised if your host continuously receives telephone calls during your meeting, it is normal, and it is not perceived to be rude, although annoying. You may find that with some clients, it is better to meet them outside the office or outside office hours in order to get their full attention.

10. Expect to spend a long time exchanging pleasantries and small talk, which if things are going well, will get into private or personal matters. Use this exchange of pleasantries to collect information about your counterpart's likes and dislikes, strengths and weaknesses and network and powerbase. All of this is normally done in the nicest possible way and is not intrusive or clearly probing.

11. Remember that creating warmth and trust must precede business, not the other way round. Most of your counterparts would want to know you well at the personal level and get to trust you before they do business. Call it an instinct or a business etiquette, but they are interested in you. Look at it this way: would you rather do business with people you can trust, or people you can sue?

12. If you manage to achieve all your targets on the first meeting, you have done well. You will find this will be true with very busy or Westernised people. However, it is more normal that the business will get done over several meetings, so allow for this, and don't get frustrated.

13. Remember that the host/guest dynamics in the Arab culture will also be valid in the business world (more about that later). You may choose to visit people on certain occasions, but on others, it may be advantageous if you are the one being visited.

14. Meetings outside the office environment are common, and business will be discussed and concluded just the same as in the office. Whatever you do, avoid the Going Dutch tradition which is perceived as being abhorrent in the Arab and Chinese cultures.

15. Whilst agendas are common within certain official circles and at senior levels, not everything on the agenda will be discussed, and not everything discussed would be on the agenda. Agendas serve to direct the meeting, not to restrict it. Digressions are accepted, and surprises are common.

16. Note-taking varies according to the level of seniority and degree of complexity, but in the main it is not common or as detailed as it is in the West. Too much emphasis on taking notes will inevitably undermine the verbal and personal contact, and it may show distrust. However, do feel free to write down headings or take note of complex figures or technical details.

17. Sending memos or summaries after important meetings is not common but it is a good idea for you to take the initiative here to clarify understanding on both sides. It is sometimes your only record of what went on during the meeting. If you wait for their record of the meeting, you may never receive it.

18. Conclusions, agreements, summaries or action points may not be flagged, sign-posted or structured in the way you are used to. They may be raised in the last few minutes whilst you are getting ready to leave. It is important that you take the initiative to create commitment.

19. Circular agendas and frequent digressions may serve to maintain a friendly atmosphere and help create an holistic approach, but they may also be deliberate enough to distract you, so you need to strike a balance between circularity and linearity.

20. Going with the circular flow of typical meetings is one thing, but keep your eye on the ball and don't lose sight of your objectives. One tip is to memorize the key issue or points you want to raise during the meeting and limit them to a manageable number.

21. A good sense of timing and the need not to rush things where possible will go a long way in creating a good impression and maintaining harmony. However, make sure that you set realistic deadlines, and stick to them. After all, your ability to deliver is a bottom line here.

22. If you are visiting the area for few days or longer, make sure that you can extend your visit where necessary. Don't allow time, or lack of it, to become your Achilles heel. Expect that you will be heavily entertained, and make sure you reciprocate appropriately when they visit you back home.

23. Large meetings with several people from each side may serve many purposes, but they have pitfalls. Decisions are rarely made during these meetings, and hierarchy can easily undermine dynamics. Try lobbying individuals before-hand so they are all ready to agree during the meeting.

24. Board and committee meetings are not there to take decisions, but to approve decisions that have already been made. Lobbying and behind the scenes meetings are vital to ensure the success of board or committee meetings.

25. Where possible and where appropriate, keep visiting clients and having meetings with them, even if there is no business to discuss. For good or bad, social meetings during office hours are common, and people will be slightly annoyed if you only visit them when you want something or when something is wrong.

26. As a general rule, do not place too many meetings close to each other. Allow for delays in starting the meeting and for late finishes. Better to waste time between meetings than turn up late.

27. If a meeting is going well, your client or counterpart is responding well, and it so happens that you are making real progress, it will go on for a long time, and you may overrun. Better to cancel your next meeting than cut the flow of the meeting in its prime.

28. During routine meetings, do not give too many concessions at an early stage. Wait until you are clear about where your counterpart stands, and be sure that for every concession you give, you will be getting one in return.

29. Whether your meeting was long or short, friendly or hostile, a success or a failure, it is always a good idea to follow it up with a telephone call to repair damage, consolidate success or confirm understanding.

30. Be prepared to use your existing network of business contacts to help you set up meetings with new clients and customers. It is often the quickest and most effective way of expanding. Ask your acquaintances about who you should see or whether they know someone else who may be interested in your product or services.

DOING BUSINESS AND NEGOTIATING

Negotiation has a lot to do with the nature of your product, its uniqueness, the balance of power, information gathering and your relationship with the client. However, there are certain tactics that you can use or that can be used against you, and hence your awareness of them will enhance your ability to improve conditions for yourself and company.

The following remarks and tips are designed to help you out. However, you will notice that there are a lot fewer tips in this section than the previous two sections. The reason is that the subject here is more complex and both negotiations and doing business depend on many factors, such as your organization's size, type of industry, market position, competition and range of products. It is a subject that lends itself a lot more to training and consultancy than generic outlines.

1. Prior to doing business or negotiating with anyone, it is a great idea if you can establish a potential mediator or arbitrator. This is someone who can help both parties reach a solution should communications terminate or if both parties cannot see eye to eye. The importance of the mediator or arbitrator can never be underestimated in collective cultures where relationships and networking mean everything.

2. If you are working with large organizations or government bodies, it is good to take stock of who your real friends and enemies are within those organizations. Factionalism is extremely common in large organizations, and it gets worst when corruption is involved. There could also be many power bases with whom you need to win favours to guarantee smooth business.

3. As frustrating as it may sound, in the Arab world, everything is negotiable. Expect that people will question every aspect of your package, product, service or offer. It is a mindset that will negotiate no matter how good the deal may be. Be prepared to absorb such a stance and try to show flexibility, creativity and patience.

4. In most collective cultures, you may find that the decision-makers may not appear until late during the negotiations. It means that you ought to ensure that you still have some concessions for the decision-maker. In other words, try to pace your concessions, and start as tough as you can.

5. Being able to show steel is important throughout the negotiation process. Walking out of meetings or at least terminating meetings is the next best thing to showing dissatisfaction or indicating the need for each party to seriously reconsider their position. In negotiations almost any tactic is permissible, with the exception of causing someone to lose face. Making people wait, using the opposition to put pressure on you and using personal pleas are common tactics, so beware.

6. Bluffing and enlarging the pie are commonly used tactics that will be used to squeeze more concessions out of you. Don't give concessions on the basis of what people are prepared to offer in the future, but rather on what is being offered right now in front of you.

7. A good relationship with your counterpart is critical for ensuring flexibility and for improving what is already a good deal. However, a good relationship will not, on its own, compensate you or your counterpart for what is essentially a bad deal. Don't stretch the relationship to a breakpoint by making unreasonable demands.

8. Although Waasta or Ma'arifa (similar to the Western old boy network – see Chapter 10) is still widespread

throughout the region, do not overstretch people's willingness to help you. Do your homework before you ask for help and use it only to open the door or to speed things up. You don't want to be in a position that causes your counterpart to lose face in trying to help you.

9. In most power distant or hierarchical societies you won't get a senior manager or official to strike or conclude a deal with someone who is several ranks below them. Make sure that you have the right people to negotiate with senior officials.

10. Delegation and empowerment in high power distant cultures is almost non-existent, and if you plan to implement such a system within your own organization then you have to allow a lot of time for people to accept taking responsibility. Most of your employees are used to passing the buck rather than accepting responsibility and sometimes loss of face.

An Arab Perspective

THE ARAB WORLD

The Arab world is a vast region that extends from Morocco in North Africa to Oman on the Arabian Sea covering over 4000 miles in distance and with a population of nearly 300 million people. The Arab world is also a term that refers to all the Arabic-speaking countries that are members of the **Arab League** and more than anything else, the term embodies many socio-cultural characteristics, historic connotations and aspirations.

The objective of this chapter is to give you some appreciation of the countries and regions that fall under the umbrella of the Arab world. In this respect, there are five key facts that need to be highlighted:

1. There is a tremendous feel of homogeneity that exists across the Arab world that defies logic, given its size, population and number of countries.

2. There is nevertheless a degree of diversity that is significant in political and economic terms, and to a lesser extent in cultural terms.

3. *The Arab Way* as this book is entitled is suggestive of thought systems and patterns of behaviour that are prevalent throughout the Arab world but there are some exceptions with certain minorities and in remote parts.

4. Arab politics, economics and modern history are sufficiently complex subjects which are of great importance to any reader on the region but they are outside the scope of this book.

5. Whilst the Arab world is undergoing a period of transition in political, economic and to a lesser extent cultural terms, I believe that many of the issues raised in this book will remain valid, irrespective of the outcome of these changes.

Against the above background, the following sections will attempt to highlight the key features that characterise the Arab world in terms of asking a number of key questions. What is the Arab League? What is the Arab world? Who are the Arabs? What are the sources of unity and diversity?

THE ARAB LEAGUE

The **Arab League** was formed after the Second World War (1945) as a socio-political organizations whose aim is **to sponsor and encourage further integration and complementarity between its member states**. It reflected very strong feelings of Arab Nationalism which were widespread at the time because many Arab countries were struggling for independence from colonial powers such as Great Britain, France and Italy. Today, the Arab League continues to play an important role in attempting to regulate relations between the Arab world and the rest of the world, as well as playing a role in inter-Arab disputes. Another important role which is played by the Arab League is to sponsor and guide many Pan-Arab organizations and initiatives concerning trade, culture, commerce and so on. The table below contains all the member countries in the Arab League.

Arab League - Member Countries

No.	Member Country	No.	Member Country
1.	Algeria	12.	Morocco
2.	Bahrain	13.	Oman
3.	Comoros	14.	Palestine
4.	Djibouti	15.	Qatar
5.	Egypt	16.	Saudi Arabia
6.	Jordan	17.	Somalia
7.	Iraq	18.	Sudan
8.	Kuwait	19.	Syria
9.	Lebanon	20.	Tunisia
10.	Libya	21.	United Arab Emirates
11.	Mauritania	22.	Yemen

The total population of the Arab world is estimated to be approaching 300 million people, and the majority of those tend to live in North Africa. Indeed, the four Arab countries where nearly 50 percent of the population lives are Egypt,

Algeria, Sudan and Morocco. With the exception of Algeria, these countries are some of the poorest Arab countries. In contrast, the richest Arab countries where you have the least population density are Saudi Arabia, United Arab Emirates, Kuwait and Qatar. Many of these counties rely on foreign labour in addressing imbalances between wealth and population. Another key characteristic that bedevils most of the Arab world is the high percentage of youth. Indeed, it is estimated that up to 60 percent of the Arab population is under the age of 24 years, and to this extent, unemployment is a key challenge to many Arab countries and it is likely to continue to be so for many years to come. Another key challenge that is faced by many Arab governments lies in their ability to implement democratic reforms to their systems whilst maintaining some form of stability.

SOURCES OF UNITY

When we talk about the Arab world we are also referring to all those countries whose official language is Arabic. The importance of the Arabic language stems from the fact that it is the language of the Koran which is the Muslim holy book and main religious source. Language is also the medium through which ideas, experiences and aspirations are shared and exchanged creating a form of cultural unity that is rare in today's world. Arab nationalism where it exists aspires that this cultural unity will one day be translated into some form of political unity.

The Arabic language is interesting in that it exists in two levels. Firstly there is the written or the formal or modern

Arabic language that is the official and media language and it is largely understood by most literate people. Secondly, there are the various dialects that are spoken and understood by everyone who ascribes to this dialect. In the majority of Arab countries, the distance between local dialects and the formal language is not necessarily that great, and some dialects are more widely understood than others. Indeed, the Egyptian dialect is the most universally understood by Arabs throughout the region given the influence of Egyptian music and films in Arab media.

In the modern world, this cultural unity is interpreted in the presence of many pan-Arab organizations that tend to address the Arab world as a whole thus maintaining a sense of cultural and linguistic unity that transcends national differences. Media is a prime example where there are now numerous satellite stations that attract Arab audiences from across the region, irrespective of dialects. Indeed, the importance of Arab media today is that it is constantly bridging many of the linguistic colloquial gaps that used to exist in the region, thus having a positive impact on Arab convergence.

The second source of unity is Islam. Although not all the Arabs are Muslims, the great majority of them are, and Islam in this respect shapes people's mindsets and opinions at a very deep level in addition to being responsible for many of the behavioural patterns that can be observed throughout the region. Whether we are looking at food and drink, dress code or attitudes, we will always find that Islam plays a fundamental role in creating a type of unity that is observed throughout the region.

Finally, most Arabs tend to perceive themselves as belonging to a great civilisation that had for eight centuries played a leading role in human history. The Arab-Islamic civilisation that flourished from the 7th century until the 15th century is a source of inspiration for many Arabs as it represents the Golden Age that most people want to recapture.

To this extent, Arabness or what makes an Arab is not a question of race but rather a question of language and mindset. It is said that an Arab is someone who thinks like an Arab, irrespective of their descent. Indeed, Arab history suggests that the Arab world is a melting pot for many races and ethnic groups that have adopted the Arabic language as their medium of communication, and for the greatest majority Islam as the main source of religious values.

The geographic position of the Arab world at the crossroads between Asia, Africa and Europe has had a dramatic effect on Arab history, culture and fortunes. The region has been invaded from all directions throughout the ages, with each conqueror leaving a mark on the landscape and culture. Travel round the Arab world, and you will see Roman amphitheatres, Greek temples, Umayyad palaces, Persian irrigation channels, Mamluki Mosques, Turkish schools, Crusader Castles and Portuguese forts.

At the same time, whilst the Arabian peninsular forms the homeland of the Arab nation, many of the countries that form part of the Arab world today have become Arabized through the course of history. This process of Arabization started before Islam in countries such as Iraq and Syria, but was accelerated by the Islamic conquests in the 7th and 8th centuries to extend to Morocco in the west. Beyond the Arabic language and the influence of Islam, the Arabization process was also accelerated by the intermarriages and alliances that were created between Arab conquerors and the indigenous populations across the region. Science and centres of learning also played a significant role in creating this Arabization throughout ages, and the most notable of these are the Umayyad Mosque in Syria, the Al-Azhar University in Egypt, Al Zaytuna University in Tunisia and Al Qarawiyeen Mosque in Morocco. Nonetheless, there remains a great deal of diversity that exists throughout the region and will be discussed later.

The Arab World

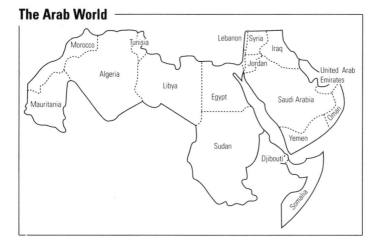

TERMS OF REFERENCE

In historic terms, the Arab world has an eastern wing called **Al-Mashrek Al-Arabi (Arab East)** and a western Wing called **Al-Maghreb Al-Arabi (Arab West)**. Al-Maghreb refers to all the countries west of Egypt, and its modern equivalent is **North Africa**. It includes **Libya, Tunisia,**

Algeria, **Morocco** and **Mauritania**. **Al-Mashrek** includes **Egypt** and all those countries east of it. The nearest modern equivalent to this is the **Middle East** although the Middle East includes Iran and Turkey, which are non-Arab.

There are clearly a number of distinctions that separate Al-Mashrek from Al-Maghreb and one of the most important ones is dialect. The various dialects that exist in that region are very different from those elsewhere. The most difficult dialect of all is the Algerian dialect as it has many French words in it followed by Tunisian dialect. Another very important distinction is the indigenous and African flavour that colours and enriches the cultures of these countries in a way that is totally absent elsewhere. More about that later.

Another commonly used regional term is the **Levant**, and this refers to what Arabs have historically defined as **Greater Syria**, which includes **Syria**, **Lebanon**, **Palestine** and **Jordan**. The term **Fertile Crescent** also refers to the Greater Syria whilst on some occasions you will come across **Mesopotamia**, which actually refers to **Iraq**. The **Arabian Peninsular** refers to **Yemen**, **Saudi Arabia**, **United Arab Emirates**, **Oman**, **Kuwait**, **Qatar** and **Bahrain**. The last six countries are members of the **Gulf Co-operation Council (GCC)**. The remaining Arab countries that are members of the Arab league are **Sudan**, **Djibouti**, **Somalia** and the **Comoro Islands**.

The position of Sudan, Djibouti and Somalia in Eastern Africa makes them, in the eyes of many people, both Arab and African simultaneously. It is difficult in those circumstances to decide whether the Arab content of these cultures is more pronounced than the African content or vice versa. To this extent, and in particular with reference to Djibouti and Somalia, there are those who would argue that the Arabness of these countries is more due to political reasons than cultural reasons. However, the fact remains that many of the issues raised in this book will remain applicable to large sectors of those societies regardless of their Arabness or lack of it.

Each of the above regional breakdowns has a historic, political or a cultural connotation. The extent to which there are variations across the region is a very interesting subject that can form the basis of another book. In this book however, and for the purposes of simplicity, we are more interested in the commonalities that exist rather than the differences. However, the following two sections will attempt to highlight the sources of diversity within the region.

THE ARAB PEOPLES

Any historic review of the Arab world would be incomplete without reference to the enormous impact other cultures have had on the Arab culture. The Arab world can easily be described as the original cross-cultural melting pot where various cultures and civilizations have left their mark on the Arab mosaic whether it be in dialects, jewellery, architecture, food, arts and crafts, dress, music and values. As shown in the diagram on the next page, these cross-cultural influences have come from all directions and they have also been present throughout history.

The richness of the Arab culture lies in its ability to absorb other cultural influences without losing its own cultural identity. If you travel to many Gulf states, you will definitely feel both the Indian and Persian influences in many aspects of traditional life, such as food, jewellery and architecture. In the case of Oman, you will also feel the African influence in Omani music, crafts and dress.

Travel to Syria and Lebanon, and you won't be able to escape the Turkish and sometimes European influences. In Egypt, you will not only feel the African influences but also the Turkish influence as seen in the grand mosques and palaces of Cairo. Take Morocco, and you will find that Moroccan or Andalusian architecture is a fine synthesis of Arabic, African and Gothic Architecture.

Cross-Cultural Influences

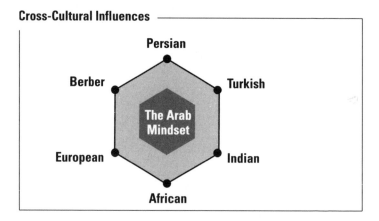

Within the Arab world, there remain a great number of ethnic groups who for a variety of historic and cultural reasons were not wholly absorbed into the main body of the Arab culture or they were not wholly Arabized. In the Al-Mashrek, the most notable of these groups are the Kurdish people of Iraq and Syria who, although they share many attributes of the Arab culture, have retained many other cultural features pertaining to language, dress-code and food. The same can be said about smaller numbers of Armenians, Turkish and Caucasian minorities that are particularly settled in the Fertile Crescent and Iraq. Within Egypt and Sudan, there are the Nubians who are becoming more vocalized in demanding recognition of their indigenous cultures.

Politically, the most pronounced ethnic groups in the Arab world are the Berbers of North Africa. The Berbers or the Amazighs (Noble People) are the indigenous population of North Africa and many aspects of their culture have survived many centuries of Arab civilization, and the more extreme groups of the Berbers remain very resistant to Arab influences. The Amazighs of North Africa have many dialects and their presence is mostly felt in Algeria, especially in the eastern parts where they are highly politicized. The degree of their politicization is as dependent on the governments attempts to marginalize their culture as it is on French influence and particularly the Francophonic elements within the Amazigh population. During the French colonization of Algeria and as part of a French policy of divide and rule, the French authorities did everything to win favours with the Amazighs, who are now paying the price post independence.

Another equally pronounced group exists in the Mashrek in the form of the Kurdish population of Iraq and Syria. Today, many Kurdish people who also exist in Turkey and Iran have aspirations of independence. Their dream of an independent nation has recently been revived given the present situation in Iraq where much hope is placed on the support of the USA in return for aiding it in its policies towards Iraq. However, the fact that the Kurdish people are dispersed over four countries and a future state will be land-locked and thus dependent on the goodwill of those four countries are the most important factors militating against the emergence of an independent Kurdish nation.

Notwithstanding the above, and when examining cultural traits of the Amazighs and the Kurdish people, I am satisfied that although they have many legitimate political aspirations, they continue to share many cross-cultural traits with their Arab neighbours. I recall one incident where I gave a 20-point summary on the Arab culture to a highly militant Amazigh activist to see whether it applied to Amazighs and he returned it with one basic correction. He replaced the word Arab with Amazigh every time it occurred in the text.

THE LEVELS OF DIVERSITY

To sum up from the previous section, we have to imagine that the value systems in the Arab World exist at three levels (see the diagram opposite). At the most basic and fundamental level, there are essentially many cultural values that bind the Arab World together and which I call **Pan Arab Values**. These include the role and importance of hospitality, the Arabic language (excluding dialects), family values, historic outlook, architecture and most importantly Islam. This book is mainly concerned with the Pan Arab Values although some reference will be made to regional and national values.

However, when we look at the Arab World from a regional point of view we begin to see regional differences or variations that emerge as a result of historic, economic or geographic factors. For example, it is difficult to overlook the

Turkish influence in countries such as Syria, Iraq or Algeria whether we are looking at food, architecture or language. It is equally difficult to ignore Persian influence on Iraqi and Gulf life, dialects, culture and arts. Finally, at the national level, if we take the Algerian war of independence, there is every indication that it has shaped the Algerian mindset in a way that is extremely different from say Tunisia on the one side and Morocco on the other. These variations, whilst being very important, fall outside the scope of this book.

The Arab Peoples

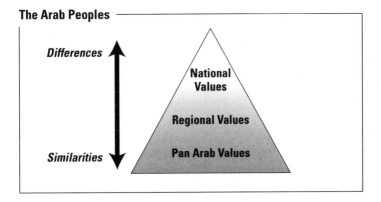

THE ARABIC LANGUAGE

The Arabic language is the language of the Koran and as such it is revered to the extent that Muslims have an obligation to preserve it on the one side whilst continuing to develop it on the other. Indeed, there are many national and regional organizations and institutions throughout the Arab World whose duty is to protect and oversee the usage, teaching and development of the Arabic language at the official and commercial levels. Furthermore, poetry continues to play a central role in Arab daily life and it is often said that poetry is the book of the Arabs. To this extent, linguistic eloquence is always appreciated by Arabs, whereby style and delivery can be as important as content. Finally, the Arabic language is what brings the Arab World and culture together as was suggested by Sir James Craig (1997) when he noted:

The refusal of the Arabic language to split up is proof of the importance of language in the Arab mind and in the Arab world. Arabic has not split up because Arabs attach importance to it not only as a tool of communication but as a symbol. And Arabic has not split up because the Arabs did not themselves want to split up...

One of the most important characteristics of the Arabic language is its comprehensiveness. It is said that with the Arabic language's intrinsic system of derivation that relies on derivation from mainly 3-letter roots, the language can potentially expand to one million words. This makes it an enormous language by world standards and more importantly, able to absorb many of the new scientific and technical discoveries and concepts that the West throws at it. It is important to remember that for nearly eight centuries, the Arabic language was the scientific language of civilisation and its books on science, geography, literature and philosophy were translated to many European languages.

Another important feature of the Arabic language is that it is a poetical language in a very big way. I can think of no other language or culture where poetry and eloquence continue to be a permanent feature in everyday life than in the Arab world. In everyday use, the language is full of idioms, euphemisms, proverbs and flowery phrases that will baffle and sometimes confuse most foreigners. This love of poetry and eloquence is combined with an educational system that relies heavily on rote learning as a main teaching tool. To this extent, the Arabs have a very advanced memory system that will astound most foreigners, whether it be in remembering incidents from a long time ago or in terms of relying on memory during meetings and lectures. Finally, most Westerners will note that when Arabs communicate in writing, their language tends to be both elaborate and formal, which can send conflicting messages to the untrained reader.

LEARNING THE LANGUAGE

I am frequently asked by departing expatriates *'Do we need to learn Arabic?'* The short answer is 'not always'. Most educated Arabs speak English, and in the case of North Africa and Lebanon, French is widely spoken. However, once you are away from main cities, you will find that basic knowledge of Arabic will come in handy. Notwithstanding this, I strongly advice people to learn basic Arabic phrases and greetings as a matter of courtesy to the people you are living amongst.

I was once visiting a middle manager in an Arab ministry when a Korean Engineer approached him and started speaking in a mixture of broken Arabic and English. I noticed that the official was bending backwards to help him in every way he could, even though I knew that both the official and the Korean engineer could speak English a lot better than the Arabic being spoken. When the Korean engineer left, I asked my host why he had persisted in speaking Arabic with the visitor and whether he considered it to be important. The official's answer was that as the Korean had made the effort to speak Arabic, he felt it was important to encourage his development and appreciated it to the extent that he would help him more than others who could not be bothered to even utter a few words in Arabic.

The moral of the story is that the more visitors try to learn about Arabic and the Arabic culture, the more it will be appreciated by Arabs, who will consider it a pleasure to help them. It is the most natural human reaction the world over.

For most Europeans, Arabic is a difficult language to learn. However, one needs to make a distinction between spoken or colloquial Arabic and literary or classic Arabic. Spoken Arabic varies regionally, and thereby you will need to learn the dialect of the country you are visiting. There is no use trying to master the Moroccan dialect if you plan to live in Saudi Arabia. The most commonly understood regional dialect in the Arab world is the Egyptian dialect given the prevalence of Egyptian films and music.

Whilst spoken Arabic is useful for holding short conversations, asking for directions or bargaining in the Souks, you will need literary Arabic to be able to read the newspapers, or company reports and so on. Whereas you will need one or two weeks to learn basic spoken Arabic, you will need to persevere for at least three months to learn literary Arabic. Finally, whilst spoken Arabic can be specific to a country or region, literary Arabic is universal in the entire Arab World.

LEARNING TIPS

Generally speaking, there are now plenty of intensive language training programmes, which, although expensive, are both effective and time efficient. If you decide to attend one of those programmes, my advice is to insist on a pre-course pack where you can learn, in your own time, basic things such as numbers, the alphabet, greetings and so on. This will save you plenty of precious time during the programme itself.

The absolute minimum duration I would recommend is one week, but whatever duration you choose my advice is to have a break in the middle where you can go away and consolidate what you have learnt. Indeed, even on a one-week programme most people reach the saturation stage after three days.

Furthermore, it is good practice to tape record some modules with your tutor, including mistakes and corrections, which you can listen to later. Also, take every opportunity to practise your Arabic with Arab colleagues even though it is going to be slow. Finally, it has been my experience that few people have the discipline and persistence to learn languages on their own using 'teach yourself' books. Nevertheless, if you only want to learn basic phrases and greetings, then there are plenty of good phrasebooks about, but make sure you buy the right book for the country you are visiting.

When you first learn Arabic and depending on what level you reach, you will find that people's reactions vary tremendously. If you are still at a stuttering stage after one week of intensive language training, the reaction will be of amusement, but if you are too slow, people will be very keen to help you out. Other people won't have the patience to wait while you are searching for the right word, and unfortunately they will switch into English.

If you reach a proficient level after three to six months of training, you are likely to be able to hold a half hour conversation with no trouble. Most people will be delighted to listen to you and correct you where possible or at least suggest language shortcuts to help you out. But even after three months of training, you won't be able to do everything in Arabic, this will take years. It will take you an even longer time to be able to understand various dialects especially if you find yourself in the Arab Gulf states where there are many Arab expatriates from across the region.

Whatever you decide to do, perseverance is critical and a good sense of humour will come in handy when you are making mistakes.

TRANSLATING INTO ARABIC

Arabic is a very beautiful, expressive and poetic language. To start with, Arabic calligraphy is substantial and the style you choose will add to your corporate image if that is a concern. There are many good examples where international companies have managed to create a level of synergy between the Latin and Arabic scripts. Do take your time in choosing the right script for your corporate image. A good translator will be able to offer you over 50 scripts to choose from. Once you have chosen that script, offer it to Arab colleagues or dealers to gather their opinion before going to print.

Furthermore, there are certain words or concepts that are not immediately translatable and you may need to find a good and creative translator or copywriter who is able to preserve your key message but without being too literal. It is incredible that some organizations will be willing to spend a lot of money to choose the right wording in their own language but are unwilling to do so when it comes to translation. It is not courtesy to the language to send your literature out in bad Arabic, and it will reflect badly on you.

Also, with visual images, do remember that Arabs read from right to left. This means that if you have a sequence of photos you need to order them from right to left and not from left to right as you would do in Western cultures. The same applies when you are combining text and graphics where you have to be absolutely sure whether it is the text or the graphics you want the reader to read first.

Finding a good translator is not as easy as most people think. Unfortunately, it is common practice in most Western countries for any person to call themselves a translator without necessarily having the qualification to do the job properly. You need to work with professional organizations, and it is my experience that translations carried out in the Arab world tend to be of better quality and on the whole cheaper. Check with your agents or Arab colleagues if you can translate in their own country. The bottom line here is that no translation is better than a bad translation. A bad translation shows lack of respect for the language and could even be considered insulting. If you do decide to translate through a professional organization make sure you get it edited by a third party.

Finally, do remember that if you are translating into Arabic in a written format, then whatever you translate for one market, say Egypt, will on the whole be good enough for another market, such as Morocco. The same, however, does not apply if you are producing a video that relies on spoken Arabic. You might find it difficult to use a video that was made in Tunisia for use in Jordan. This is the time where you will need independent advice.

SOME USEFUL PHRASES

◆ The most universal greeting throughout the Arab and Islamic world is **As-Salaam Alaikum** meaning **Peace Be Upon You** and the answer to the greeting is **Wa Alaikum As-Salaam** meaning **And upon you Be Peace**. It can be used anytime of the day both formally and informally and in writing or over the telephone.

◆ **Marhaba** is a common greeting that can be used in some of Al-Mashrek countries and it is equivalent to **Hello** and the answer is **Marhabtain** meaning **Two Hellos**. It is most common amongst Jordanians, Palestinians, Lebanese and Syrians.

◆ **Sabah El-Kheir** means Good Morning and the answer is **Sabah El-Noor**. Good Afternoon does not exist in Arabic whilst **Good Evening** is **Masaa' El-Kheir** and the answer is **Masaa' El-Noor**. All of these phrases are common across the region.

- **Ahlan Wa Sahlan** is the phrase that Arabs use to greet you when you visit them, meaning Welcome. The answer is **Ahlan Beek** if responding to a man and **Ahlan Beeki** if responding to a woman.

- Arabs also use the phrase **Tafadhal** if they are ushering you to their office, handing you a cup of tea or coffee or inviting you to start eating. It means **Do Me the Honour**, and if you are addressing a lady you add 'i' at the end, and if you are addressing a group you add 'oo'.

- The word for Thank You in Arabic is **Shokran** but sometimes people will use **Mashkoor** (Gulf) **Mutshakir** (Egypt) if the speaker is a man and **Mashkooreh** or **Mutshakireh** if the speaker is a woman. The answer is **Afwan**, which actually mans **Pardon Me**.

- **Ma' Es-Salaameh** or **Salaam** means **Goodbye** and you answer with the same. Another Gulf version is **Fi Amaan Illah**, and again, you answer with the same.

- **Inshaalah** means **God Willing**, and is said on many occasions, but ultimately, it relates to giving promises for the future.

- There are many words for **How Are You** such as **Keif Haalak** or **Keifak** in the Levant, **Shlawnak** in the Gulf and **Izzayak** in Egypt. If you are addressing a female, you simply substitute the 'ak' at the end with 'ek', and if you are addressing a group of people, you substitute the 'ak' with 'kum'.

◆ A very common answer to 'How are you?' is **Al-Hamdulilah** meaning **Thanks Be to God**. You can also answer with **Bekheir Shokran** meaning **In Good Form Thank You**. You can also answer with **Tamaam Shokran** meaning **Good Thank You**. **Tamaam** also means **Perfect**. You can substitute Tamaam with either **Zein** (Gulf) or **Kuwayyis** (Egypt and Levant) both meaning **Fine**. However, if you are a woman you have to add 'eh' to both Zein and Kuwayyis.

◆ **Ma'alaish** is commonly used to mean **Never mind** or **don't upset yourself** or to ask you to **calm down**.

◆ **Yallah** when said with a hand sweep can also mean never mind, but if used alone it can mean **Let's Go**, and if said twice it means **Hurry** or **Make a Move**.

◆ There are many words for **Yes** such as **Na'am**, **Ayweh**, **Eeh** with the first being the most formal. The word for **No** is **La'** with a glottal stop at the end. You will sometimes hear the phrase **Mush Mumkin** meaning **Not Possible** and **Laazim** meaning **You Must**.

ARABIC NUMBERS

1.	Waahad	21.	Waahad Wu Eshreen
2.	Ethnein	22.	Ethnein Wu Eshreen
3.	Thalaatheh	23.	Thalaath Wu Eshreen
4.	Araba'ah	24.	Arba'ah Wu Eshreen
5.	Khamseh	30.	Thalaatheen
6.	Sitteh	31.	Waahad Wu Thalaatheen
7.	Sab'ah	32.	Ethnein Wu Thlaatheen
8.	Thamaanyeh	35.	Khamseh Wu Thalaatheen
9.	Tis'ah	40.	Arba'een
10.	Asharah	50	Khamseen
11.	Ehda'esh	60.	Sitteen
12.	Ethna'esh	70.	Sab'een
13.	Thalaath Taesh	80.	Thamaaneen
14.	Arba' Taesh	90.	Tis'een
15.	Khames Taesh	100.	Miyeh
16.	Sitt Taesh	101.	Miyeh Wu Waahad
17.	Saba' Taesh	200.	Miyetain
18.	Thaman Taesh	300.	Thalaath Miyeh
19.	Tisa' Taesh	400.	Arba' Miyeh
20.	Eshreen	1000.	Alf

First Encounters
with Arabs

CULTURAL QUIZ

Examine the following statements below and mark whether you think they are true or false. Don't spend more than five minutes in total.

1. You must always take a gift with you when visiting Arab friends.
2. It is customary to pay compliments to your host on personal items.
3. Guests must always accept the first drink offered to them.
4. The Arab world is a multicultural and multiracial society.
5. It is customary to shake hands every time you meet Arab friends.
6. If you are presented with a gift, you must open it at once.
7. You must always present your business card with your left hand.

8. It is customary to use first names with Arabs, and titles are frowned upon.

9. You must never show the soles of your shoes in front of Arabs.

10. Pleasantries and small talk is a very important ritual to Arabs, even in business.

11. You must always avoid strong eye contact with Arabs, it is confrontational.

12. Flattery and personal praises are respected in the Arab world.

13. Pausing and silence are respected when negotiating with Arabs.

14. You must avoid talking about religion and politics to Arab colleagues.

15. It is customary for Arab women to walk five paces behind their husbands.

Answers:
1. Not true at all, but you can do if you so wish.
2. Not true at all, and try to avoid it.
3. Not true, as it is indication that you don't wish to impose.
4. Absolutely true in several ways.
5. Absolutely true, the Arab culture is a very tactile culture.
6. Not true at all, unless the giver asks you to do so.
7. Not true at all, and avoid using your left hand when interacting with people.
8. Very true, and get used to using your first name too.
9. Absolutely true, so avoid it whenever you can.
10. Absolutely true, and they can take a long time.
11. Not true except when you are dealing with members of the opposite sex.
12. Generally true, but up to a limit where flattery is not false.
13. Not true and silence must be avoided where possible.
14. Not true, but watch out if your views are in direct contrast to your counterpart.
15. Not true at all, and it is a fallacy that is propagated in movies.

BEFORE YOU TRAVEL

1. Make sure that your passport is valid for more than six months. Depending on your nationality, there are some countries where you do not need a visa, or you can pick it up at the airport. In either case, do check with the embassy or travel agent. Most visas will be valid for one month and renewable for a second month.

2. Make sure that you are up to date on the injections you need to have prior to departure, your doctor or travel agent will be able to advise you on which you need. Opinions do sometimes vary, so make sure you receive the best medical advice on this subject.

3. If you are relocating to the region, ensure that you have all the official papers plus two extra copies for good measure. Extra papers that you may need are marriage certificates, children's school certificates, university papers and, where necessary, medical reports. You never know when are you going to need them.

4. If you are travelling to the region for the first time and especially to settle there, it is always a good idea to ensure that someone is meeting you at the airport. Most reputable companies will have a good public relations officer to do that job, and if they are good, they will meet you right inside the airport.

5. Make sure that you are not carrying with you any prohibited items such as firearms, banned materials, and in a number of countries, this will include alcohol and

pork. Published materials that can be deemed to be approaching the pornographic will be confiscated and can land you in a lot of trouble, so use your discretion. In some countries, some videos will also be held for investigation, so try not to take any with you, unless they are obviously the children's type or containing family shots.

6. Prepare yourself for the hot weather by taking light (cotton) clothing and remember that in hot climates it is critical that you should drink plenty of water. However, even in the hottest countries it can turn cold at night in the winter months, or if you decide to go camping in the desert, so take something warm with you.

GETTING THERE

Personal Safety. The Arab world is generally very safe to travel to, and it has some of the lowest crime rates in the world. However, when you arrive at the airport and if you are not being met, make sure to take government licensed taxis. If in doubt, ask a policeman.

Hotels and Restaurants. Most Arab capitals will have a wide selection of international Five Star hotels, and you will be spoilt for choice. International cuisine is widely available, and there are many international style supermarkets especially in the capital cities. Most supermarkets will stock various brands of foreign food and delicacies. You will also be able to pick up international newspapers from hotels or recognized newsagents.

Working Day. The working day normally starts very early in the morning between 7.30 am and 8.00 am. Prepare yourself to be up and running by 8 am at the latest. Whilst most government offices start working by 8.00 am, do remember that in the private sector, meetings don't really begin until slightly later. The weekend is traditionally on Friday although more Arab countries are adding either Thursday or Saturday to the weekend.

Transport. Car hire is widely available but there are plenty of cheap taxis. Most taxis are now metered, although there are a few where you have to haggle. Ask a local friend or at the hotel what kind of fare you should be paying. If you are travelling between cities, public transport could come in the form of shared taxis or busses. Trains are not common.

Cash and Credit Cards. All major credit cards are accepted in hotels and large shops, but there are occasions when you have to pay more if you are using a credit card. This is true in the traditional markets (Souks) and especially on items such as jewellery and carpets. You can withdraw cash from local cash-points although the exchange rates may not be to your liking.

Driving. The standards of driving in most Arabic cities can only be described as risky by most western standards. In some countries you can attend special driving lessons which are called defensive driving. For most westerners, you can exchange your driving license with a local one pretty easily.

Rented Accommodation. In most Arab cities you will find a wide range of rented accommodation and the standards are generally very high especially in the modern high rise buildings or villas. Prices could range tremendously across the city and you could easily find yourself paying a premium price either as a Westerner or when you insist on living in the expatriate areas.

WHAT'S IN A NAME?

Paradoxically, Arabs are on the whole fairly informal with regards to first names and reasonably formal as far as titles are concerned. This is characterised by the use of first names at all times and irrespective of the degree of familiarity. A Mr Mike Smith will be addressed as Mr Mike or simply Mike but not Mr Smith. So do remember to put emphasis on your first name and avoid using your surname as a habit or addressing people with their surnames or family names.

However, where there is a wish to maintain formality, courteous Arabs will use a variety of titles such as **Sayyid** (Mr.), **Sayyideh** (Madam), **Akh** (Brother), **Ukht** (Sister) or **Anissa** (Miss). However, do remember that in some countries the title Sayyid can be a religious title, for Shi'at Muslims specially. Western titles such as Miss and Madam are sometimes used in the Arab world especially amongst sophisticated society.

Furthermore, bear in mind that professional titles such as Doctor, Engineer and Lawyer are commonly used. The same for inherited titles such as **Sheikh** or **Amir** (sometimes written as Emir).

Make sure that your business card is informative but without being pretentious. Education, qualifications and position in the company are all too important, so don't dismiss them out of humility.

You may also come across the title **Hajji** that is sometimes used following a pilgrimage to Mekkah. However, it should be emphasized that in strict Islamic sense this is frowned upon. The titles **Sharif** and **Sayyid** refer to descendants of the Prophet Mohammed and are common in a number of Arab countries including Jordan and various Gulf States.

The name construction in the Arab world is very simple. Say you meet **Ahmed Hilal Salem Al-Mansoori**. Ahmed would be his first name (and not his Christian name), Hilal is his father's name, Salem will be his grandfather's name and Al-Mansoori is the family or tribal name. More about the meaning of **Al** later. The name construction for females follows a similar pattern where the female will inherit her father's name as a second name and so on.

Under strict Islamic laws, a women should not change her name after marriage but retains her maiden name and thus her independence. Whilst this is seen as a progressive sort of thing in some Western societies, it is a well established tradition in most Arab countries. A similar principle is used for adopted children who retain their biological father's name irrespective of who adopts them, thus automatically giving them the right to know who their parents are.

THE RULES OF FORMALITY

The most commonly used inherited title in the Arab world is **Sheikh**, which literally means old man, and it is an honorary title, which also suggests the importance of age in the Arab context. Today, the carrier of the title Sheikh need not be an old man but could be quite young.

Sheikh as a title can describe a whole range of things. To start with, it can be a religious title given to scholars. It is also a tribal title given to the head of the tribe as well as his children. In the UAE, the head of the state carries the title of Sheikh. It is also a title that is sometimes given to various dignitaries such as ministers or ex-ministers. Nonetheless, it is very rare that people will acquire such a title as a result of distinguished public service.

However, if we take Qatar and Kuwait, the head of state is known as Amir (meaning Prince and often transliterated as Emir) whilst members of the royal family carry the title of Sheikh. In Saudi Arabia, the head of the state official title is the Custodian of the Two Holy Places although he is often referred to as the King. Members of the Saudi royal family carry the title of Amir. In Oman, the head of the state is known as Sultan. Members of the Omani royal family are referred to as Sayyid whereas in Morocco they are referred to as Sidi. In Bahrain, the head of the state is now addressed as King whilst members of the royal family will carry the title Sheikh.

Outside the Arab Gulf states, the title sheikh tends to refer to a tribal head, and it is usually a hereditary title as suggested earlier. This is true for Jordan, Iraq, Syria and Lebanon. Unlike in Britain and some other European countries, there is no equivalent to Lord, Sir, Duke or Viscount. The title Sheikh does tend to sum all of these titles.

When addressing royalty or senior people, it is usual to address members of royalty as Your Majesty for a king, Your Royal Highness for a member of royal family, Your Highness for head of state and Your Excellency for senior officials.

Notwithstanding all of the above, and given the strong Bedouin tradition in most Arab countries, it is still common to refer to the head of the state only by his first name whilst in speaking or in the press. Sometimes other terms of endearment are used, thus emphasizing the egalitarian roots of the Arab culture.

UNDERSTANDING FAMILY NAMES

Surnames, family or tribal names are very rarely used during informal or verbal interaction, although they are very important in their own right. It is very unusual for an Arab to refer to a colleague by his or her surname except when used as a term of endearment, which is common in a number of North African countries. If you are addressing officials in writing, it is common to write their first and family name.

♦ You will notice that many family names will begin with **Al** which means **The**, and in some cases (Egypt) it is transliterated as **El**, and in some North African countries, it is reversed to become **Le** or **La**. The prefix **Al** and its many variations need not indicate that this is an established family although it has a feel of grandeur about it. There are well established families whose surnames do not begin with **Al**.

♦ Some family names can also begin with **Abu** meaning Father of which is common in the Fertile Crescent, and in North Africa and in the Gulf this is sometimes shortened to **Bu**. Also in some Gulf countries and Yemen you may come across **Bal** which is a combination of Father of and The (Bu + Al = Bal).

♦ In other cases, certain family names will begin with **Bin** meaning Son of which is sometimes transliterated as **Ben** in North Africa, and you may come across it as **Ibn**. In Mauritania you will also come across **Wild** as part of the surname, which also means Son of. Incidentally, **Bint** means daughter or girl or virgin.

The importance of surnames, family names or tribal names can never be underestimated. For good or bad, tribalism is still a very strong institution in the Arab world and it does play an important role in many aspects of public life. The reality is that there are leading families or tribes and there are influential ones, and there are preferred tribes and there are marginalized tribes or families.

Knowing your way around the tribal myriad in some Arab countries will be particularly helpful in choosing your partners or forming strategic alliances. Some families will control certain sectors or sub-sectors of the economy whilst other families will be dominant in a certain public sector or subsector of it. They will sometimes form the hidden powerbases who control and manipulate according to specific interests. In some other countries, tribalism is replaced with regionalism but the effects are the same. Nepotism is a way of life.

INTERPRETING BODY LANGUAGE

In most high context cultures body language is very important. As previously mentioned, if the body language conflicts with the spoken language, you should believe the body language. By body language we mean many things such as:

- the duration of the handshake, whether it is firm or soft;
- the personal space;
- the eye contact or lack of it;
- the way people are sitting or if they choose to stand instead;
- whether somebody stands up to greet you or meet you by the door;
- whether they lean forward when they are talking to you or lean back.

As in all cultures, there are dos and don'ts regarding body language, and there are standard conventions that may be confusing to non-Arabs. To start with, it is crucially important that you stand up when greeting people irrespective of your gender or theirs. Failing to stand up properly or barely standing up can sometimes be taken as an insult especially in the absence of familiarity. Whilst in the West it is a women's prerogative not to stand up, it is no one's prerogative not to stand up in the Arab world.

When relaxed in the company of a friend, it is said that some Arabs will slouch rather than sit upright, and that is acceptable amongst friends, and is not as a sign of disrespect. Leaning forward when talking to people is considered a sign of warmth whilst leaning back is interpreted as an attempt to put some distance between yourself and your counterpart.

When engaged in heated debate or discussion, Arabs have a tendency to point with their fingers, and it is not meant to be rude. Furthermore, in the Arab world it is considered bad manners to give or receive things using your left hand as well as to eat with the left hand. The left hand/right hand rules are an old tradition dating back to the desert when people, for hygienic reasons, divided the functions of the hands: the right hand for clean deeds and the left hand for dirty deeds.

Showing the soles of one feet or shoes can also be offensive, as the case may be when crossing one's legs. However, if you are invited into a traditional gathering where you may have to sit on the floor (as in desert camping) when you are sitting cross-legged you will inevitably end up showing the soles of your feet, and that is acceptable in this context. The wisdom behind this tradition is that the soles of your feet or shoes could be very dirty and so you should not place them in front of others.

ESTABLISHING EYE CONTACT

Eye contact is the most interesting aspect of body language, and it has many interpretations in different cultures. For the Arabs, the eye is the ultimate expression of beauty as it gives away too many secrets and impressions on the well-being of the individual. The eye is also a true mirror of the heart, and reflects feelings and intentions more honestly and eloquently than words.

Whereas continuous or strong eye contact is considered disrespectful or confrontational in the Japanese culture, Westerners will sometimes use eye contact to put pressure on others. In the Arab culture, it is important to maintain good eye contact in as far as looking in the direction of one's subject(s). Looking away for long periods or frequently can be interpreted as a sign of disrespect or evasiveness, looking down is a sign of embarrassment or subservience, and looking up can be interpreted as being arrogant or condescending.

Furthermore Arabs will sometimes raise their eyebrows meaning No which is often done as a form of exclamation in many European cultures. Conversely, Arabs will some times touch the side of one eye to mean, Yes, or they will place their hand on their head. Alternatively, Arabs will touch their noses with the forefinger to mean, Yes, whereas this means, keep your nose out in most European cultures.

READING THE TACTILE CULTURE

The Arab culture is very tactile, and to a point that often surprises or even embarrasses most Westerners. To start with, handshakes, which are almost compulsory and frequent, have a tendency to linger or be longer than what most Westerners are used to. In fact, a good handshake between friends can last for few minutes, and it could go on to the extent that men will walk along the street holding hands. The sexual connotations that Westerners will attach to this are simply non-existent in the Arab world. Don't be alarmed if a colleague (of the same sex) puts their arm round your shoulder or even holds your hand whilst walking, both are signs of warmth and friendship.

Associated with this is the concept of personal space. Typically, Europeans will define their personal space as being at an arm's length. For the Arab it is much smaller. People will come closer to you as a sign of trust and warmth, and the idea that they are threatening or encroaching on your space would not cross their minds. They are simply demonstrating both warmth and trust in you as a friend. However, the Arab culture is also a gender culture where the rules are different when you are meeting persons from the opposite sex. More about that in the next section.

APPRECIATING GENDER DIFFERENCES

In the Arab world gender matters in terms of everyday interaction between the two sexes. Whereas the rules explained earlier apply when people of the same sex meet and interact, some of these rules do not apply when meeting people of the opposite sex. To start with, the segregation of sexes is still a very common phenomenon throughout most Arab countries and societies. The more conservative the society is, the more we are likely to come across various types of segregation. This segregation is based on Islamic principles but is also reinforced by Arab values pertaining to the honour of the family where women are perceived to be that shield of honour. It could be said that the Arab culture is exceptionally protective of their womenfolk.

As a whole, and throughout Arab countries, you will find that the educational system tends to be segregated, especially for children above the age of 12. The rights, merits or wrongs of this policy are not the subject of discussion in this book but suffice to say that this policy of segregation tends to be popular. In the more conservative societies, the segregation extends to university education, and in some countries, there are special banks, beaches and shopping centres for women. Some ministries and public departments will even facilitate special queues for women.

Notwithstanding the above, this is a most contentious or controversial area, and one where you will notice tremendous variation across the Arab world. Some countries will be stricter than others, to the extent that it is very difficult to generalize. Indeed, the more liberal Arabs will find this section a grim introduction to the position of Arab women. However, it remains a fact that the Islamic code of dress is becoming more popular amongst Arab women than before.

When you meet an Arab for the first time of the opposite sex, do not be surprised if they refrain from shaking hands with you. If you are a male meeting an Arab female you are likely to know on the basis of dress code. If the woman is dressed in Islamic dress (Hijab) it is possible that she will refrain from shaking hands with you, but you cannot take this as a general rule. If you are a female meeting an Arab man it is a bit more difficult to guess.

Nevertheless, as a general safe rule, when you meet a person from the opposite sex for the first time, don't be the first to offer your hand, but allow them to make the first move. From this point onwards, you will know whether this person will shake hands with you or not. Instead of shaking hands, some people will put their right hand on their hearts as a form of greeting and a sign of warmth. Also try to maintain a safe distance from members of the opposite sex, and avoid strong or continuous eye contact.

INCREASING WOMEN'S ROLES

Segregation does not mean that women are excluded from public life, marginalized or oppressed as most Western media tends to portray, to the annoyance and frustration of most Arabs. The idea that Arab women should walk five paces behind their husbands is more the result of Western imagination than Arab values. The simple fact is that more and more women are going to work today and more are occupying important government positions. To give an example, in the early 1960s, there was only one school for girls in Saudi Arabia, and today there are over 2 million female students in Saudi schools and universities. Furthermore, up to a quarter of media writers in Saudi Arabia are women, and the situation is improving continuously.

Indeed, in reviewing many current developmental issues in the Arab world, it would be unfair to carry out a direct comparison with current European standards and ways of doing things. It is a lot fairer to compare what was the case say 30 years ago with what is the current situation. For some countries the last 30 years or so have witnessed tremendous changes in the socio-political and economic situation- changes that took *hundreds of years* of evolution in European countries. This is not to say that one cannot criticise lack of development in certain sectors here and there.

In addition, the extent of women's participation in the job market has now gone beyond the traditional care sectors to include banking and finance, information technology and public relations. The changing role of women throughout the Arab world means that there are an increasing number of women running their own businesses or as board members of large conglomerates. There are women's institutions in every Arab country and there is no shortage of enthusiasm for higher involvement. Finally, I have often been told by multinationals that they find it easier to employ and train women rather than men in the Arab world.

On the last point, it appears that female students in the Arab world are proving to be more than a match for male students. This is explained by the fact that many girls see education as a way out of many social restrictions and thus it acts as a key drive for them to excel at school or university – more so than the boys. It is also said that multinationals prefer women over men as the former tend to be more settled in their career choices and require much more realistic salary structures than their male counterparts.

ASPECTS OF DRESS CODE

Dress code in the Arab world varies tremendously from one country to another and from one part of the country to the other. For example, you are likely to come across more traditional dress codes the further you go away from main cities and international centres. Equally, some countries are on the whole more conservative than others, whilst some tend to be outright liberal. The two ends of the spectrum here are Saudi Arabia which is ultra conservative and Lebanon which is by comparison highly liberal.

However, on the whole the dress code tends to be conservative and there is a varying degree of emphasis on modesty. This is particularly true for many of the Arab Gulf states where they have held to their traditional or national costumes much more than many other Arab countries. In general, tight fitting, short and revealing garments for ladies are frowned upon. You will also note that this dress code is primarily for outdoors, whilst for indoors, a cursory look at the fashion shops in the Arab world will show that anything goes.

The dress code for men is also worth mentioning. Under strict Islamic principles, Muslim men are not supposed to wear gold or silk and they are certainly not expected to indulge in tight fitting or revealing clothes. In the business world, managers are expected to dress smartly and this includes wearing suits or at a least shirt and tie for men, whilst for women the rules are less restrictive as long as they remain modest.

Most Westerners will either have come across or know about the **Abaaya** which is a long loose (often black) cloak that is traditionally worn by Arab women over a long dress, and covering the head. Today, the **Hijaab** is the modern equivalent where loose fitting clothes are worn with a headscarf. Other traditional dresses include the **Thobe**, which is a long dress worn throughout Arabia. Within the Arab Gulf states, the **Thobe** is normally decorated with sequins, whereas in the Fertile Crescent, embroidery is more common, with the Palestinian national dress being the most stunning. On the whole, Arabs have absolutely no objections to Westerners trying their national dress, but seek advice first.

For men, and specifically within the Arab Gulf states, you will note that most nationals have also stuck to their national costumes which are known as **Dishdashehs**, **Thobes** or **Kandoorehs,** and which are long and mostly white garments that can vary in design according to the country. For example, in Saudi Arabia the men's Thobe will have collars whilst in Oman it will be collarless. Men in the Gulf will also wear head-dresses and whilst the dominant colour is white there are other colour variations such as the predominant Saudi red head-dress.

Values and Attitudes

THE POSITION OF HOSPITALITY

Hospitality in the Arab culture can be described as the mother of all virtues, the cornerstone of all social interactions and the raison d'être for many Arabs. To describe someone as being generous is truly the highest praise you can give that person. To the Arab mind, hospitality is not a luxury, or something that we can extend selectively but it is a must, whether the guest is a friend or foe, whether they arrive announced or suddenly, early or late. The word for hospitality in Arabic is **Karam** whilst the word for honour is **Karaameh**. Notice that the two words are linked to indicate the importance of hospitality to one's personal integrity and standing in society. In other words, hospitality is a way of life.

Arab hospitality is famous the world over due to its lavishness and the abundance of food that is presented. Whilst this is important, the essence of Arab hospitality lies elsewhere. True hospitality is when it is offered to a complete stranger, or to a foe, somebody who arrives unexpectedly, out of the blue so to speak. True hospitality is also associated with spontaneity, here and now, not later. Indeed, Arabs are great admirers of spontaneity whether it is related to hospitality, humour or even poetry. Arabs are also very particular about timing when it comes to personal gestures or hospitality.

True spontaneity is demonstrated when and if you compliment an Arab over a personal item such as a tie or an expensive watch. The Arab's most natural reaction is to offer it to you, there and then, on the spot. This offer can be simply a courteous offer which you should decline but it can equally be a genuine offer which will be repeated and you must accept. In some cases, and when the item is a very expensive one, the offer is made so as to say I trust you enough with this expensive item to the extent that I know that you will not accept it no matter how high the temptation is. Another dimension of this spontaneous hospitality is that Arabs like to give you something that is truly and genuinely personal and thus it has a higher value.

If you happen to accept an item from an Arab in the spirit of hospitality, the concept of timing means that you do not reciprocate immediately but you wait for the right timing or opportunity. This right timing may not be for weeks or months, but when you reciprocate, it has also to be spontaneous so as to mean that it has come from the heart and not from a shop. The element of timing also manifests itself when you are invited to a meal, where an Arab is more likely to wait for the perfect moment before the meal is laid down rather than wait for the appointed time and lay the meal down. This subtle difference between time and timing is critical in cross-cultural terms.

The guest-host relationship in the Arab world is also of great importance. When you invite people to your home, they honour you by coming, rather than you doing the honour by inviting them. In other words, the guest is king, and it is the role of the host or hostess to simply pamper the guests, to such an extent that the guest must never feel that they are imposing or need to ask for something. The guest is often guided to the best chair or seating area in the room, and coffee, tea or any other drink is almost immediately offered. To delay the offer of refreshments for longer than a few minutes is almost bordering on rudeness on the part of the hosts.

Seating arrangements in most typical Arab homes follow a traditional pattern. There is the **Sider** of the room which is the area that faces you directly as soon as you enter the room. At the Sider you are more likely to meet the sofa or settee and it is flanked by armchairs on both sides. Needless to say that the Sider is the most honoured place to seat the guest, and your Arab host is likely to insist that you sit at the Sider as a way of honouring you.

During large gatherings, and especially if you are visiting a senior dignitary at home, the dignitary is likely to be sitting at the Sider and the more important guests will be sitting either side of him or her. This will typically happen in a **Majlis** or **Madaafeh** (see page 138).

Furthermore, according to pure Arab tradition, and because the guest brings honour to the house, the idea that a guest should bring a gift was considered to be abhorrent or rude to the host until very recently. Today, the habit of bringing chocolates or flowers or any other symbolic gift is growing, but you will notice that Arabs will instinctively protest.

Finally, many of the rules of hospitality will apply to visiting people in their offices as much as their homes. This is shown through the insistence that you should drink something and the speed with which you are served a drink, and through some aspects of the seating arrangements. You are king as a guest and your host will do everything to make you feel welcome. There may be occasions when you should consider whether you ought to be the host or the guest depending on the tactical advantages of either.

Personal Story

I arrived in the UAE in August 1996. Together with a friend we decided to visit Liwa and left Abu Dhabi in the morning. We had a spectacular drive through the desert before arriving at Liwa. Turning right at Liwa we spotted a few camels inside a fence close to the road next to some houses. We drove up to the camels to have a look, and not being used to driving in the sand, we got stuck. I got out of the car and with my friend at the steering wheel I tried, without success, to push the car out of the sand. We gave up and standing there looking at each other we noticed an old man watching us.

He walked up to us and said: my sons will help you. They are not here, but I will send for them. Please come in. This was our first visit to an Arab home so we were both uncertain of what to expect. We entered into a room with cushions along the walls and with coffee and dates placed in the middle. We all sat down and were offered coffee. After a short time our host's three sons arrived. We went out, and after a short struggle, our car was free of the sand. My friend and I were just about to thank them for the hospitality and their help, when we were invited in for lunch. A big bowl of rice and chicken was placed in front of us and we had a lovely meal together with the father and his sons. We talked about ourselves and our colleagues in Abu Dhabi and we soon understood that our host knew many of our Arab colleagues.

After lunch we prepared to leave and after such hospitality, we were somewhat puzzled as what to do. Should we offer to pay him? Fortunately, we did not do that, as it would have been a grave insult. We thanked him for his hospitality, and saying goodbye, he offered to show us one of his three date-farms. Two of his sons showed us around and told us about date farming. We then thanked our hosts and drew away.

Being new in the UAE, this incident made a tremendous impression on me, and I feel it describes one of the very positive cultural assets of the Arab society. What hospitality! Had it been in my home country that somebody had got stuck with his car in front of my house, almost on my courtyard, I would have got irritated with the guy moving close to my house. I might have helped him to remove his car, but I would not have invited him in for lunch.

Danish Manager

SAMPLING ARABIC COFFEE

Coffee has a definite place in the Arab culture, traditions and rituals. From a puritan point of view, coffee belongs to the world of the Bedouin Arab. Typically, the Bedouin will wake up in the morning and after praying to Allah, he will start the ritual of making coffee. Coffee is roasted freshly and then it is ground to a rhythm in a wooden mortar that is known as the **Mihbash** in some countries. The coffee is then heated on a wood-fire, and topped up throughout the day. The coffeepot is known throughout the Arab world as the **Dallah**, and it takes different shapes in different regions. It is served in a small round cup called **Funjan**, which has no handles. Cardamom seeds are always added to the coffee blend, and in some countries, saffron. This Bedouin brew can be very strong or light depending on the region. However, only a small amount is usually offered in the cup.

To the Bedouin Arab, coffee is the symbol of honour and hospitality. It is often the first thing you are offered as soon as you arrive and it is the last thing you are offered before you leave. To refuse the coffee can be insulting to the host, unless you can come up with a strong excuse. Traditionally, you have to accept the first cup, and you must always take it with the right hand. If you would like another cup, you should hand it back to the pourer who will serve you with another. However, if you don't want any more, you simply and gently shake that cup sideways to indicate that you have had enough. Traditionally you are allowed up to three cups per serving session, with the exception of Saudi Arabia where you may go beyond three.

Throughout the Gulf States, Bedouin coffee is regularly served both in homes and government departments, and it is sometimes served with dates or **Halwa** (Omani sweet). Bedouin coffee is also still common amongst Jordanians and Palestinians. However, beyond these countries, Bedouin coffee is mainly served on special occasions; feasts, weddings, mournings and so on. Instead, what is commonly known as Turkish coffee is served. Unlike Bedouin coffee you are at liberty to refuse Turkish coffee if you do not have the palate for it. You will notice that in some countries they will bring water with it. This water is to clear your mouth before you start drinking the coffee and not to wash the sediments. One important tip here is that you should allow some time before you start drinking the coffee so the sediments can sink to the bottom. This coffee can be served with or without sugar. As in the Bedouin coffee the Turkish or sweet coffee is sometimes associated with some rituals, most notably weddings in the countries of the Levant. It is traditional when a man asks for the hand of his chosen woman he will visit her family with his parents and possibly other members of his family. The woman who is the subject of the visit is expected to make the coffee herself so as to test her abilities in making this delicacy.

HOSPITALITY TIPS

1. When extended invitations, Arabs may refuse at first, so as not to impose or to ensure that the invitation is truly meant. Arabs like to ensure that the invitation is genuine and from the heart before they accept. As a rule, always issue your invitations repeatedly whether you are offering tea or inviting someone to dinner. With regards to the latter, try to avoid arrangements that are too far in the future, and aim for something in a few days.

2. Generally, Arabs tend to dislike long dining functions that Westerners, particularly the French like. Arabs tend to leave shortly after they have eaten. Lunch invitations tend to be very short, prompt, and they are usually over in a very short time. Most people want to leave early for their siesta nap. Dinner invitations are longer and drawn out. Expect to be chatting for some time before dinner is served, and for people to leave a short while after they have eaten. Most Arabs don't enjoy the typical all-night standing, chatting, drinking and nibbling cocktail parties. Avoid them if possible, and expect guests to leave shortly after the function has started.

3. If you admire a small personal item (tie, watch, bracelet, etc) the Arab's most immediate reaction is to say 'it's yours'. This is what spontaneity is all about, and you are under no obligation to accept. However, if the offer is issued repeatedly, you may want to accept. On no account should you feel the obligation to reciprocate immediately. Wait for the right moment. This is about *timing* not time.

4. You must avoid Going Dutch as it flies in the face of hospitality. Just to make the Dutch happy, the Arabs sometimes refer to this arrangement as Going English. Anyway, the idea that friends enjoying a dinner out together should split the bill is abhorrent and distasteful. The right thing to do is to argue about who has the honour of paying.

5. As mentioned before, the idea of taking a gift when visiting people is becoming fashionable in the same way that birthday and anniversary parties are. If you present someone with a gift they may not open it in front of you. This is normal. As a man, be very sensitive about taking a gift to your host's wife, unless you know them well, or unless you are accompanied by your wife.

6. As a Westerner or non-Muslim be very sensitive to the subject of alcohol when entertaining Arabs at your home. Try not to offer it, and if you are likely to entertain Arab colleagues at home, make sure that your drinks cabinet is nowhere to be seen. Muslims are prohibited from drinking, buying, giving, receiving or even looking at alcohol.

7. In the more conservative Arab societies, segregation of sexes can extend to homes. As a man, when you are invited to visit an Arab home along with your family, you may or may not meet your hostess. Also expect that you may be split from the rest of your family for the rest of your visit.

8. There are many Arab Muslim homes where you must take your shoes off before entering the house, and it is considered dirty not to do so. There are no fixed rules here other than the need to be observant. Also expect your host to direct you to the precise spot where they want you to sit, as it will be the most comfortable.

9. When walking through a door Arabs may insist that you go first as a sign of respect to you, and you may feel the need to reciprocate. However, a good rule of thumb relating to situations whereby people cannot agree who should go first, is to favour the person standing on the right.

10. Always remember that the guest is king. Don't get too worried about making mistakes, as you will be forgiven. If you have a problem with a colleague, be the one to visit them in their offices or homes, and if you want to handle a delicate matter, it may be better to do it as a guest, rather than on neutral ground.

11. Corporate gifts are big business throughout the Arab world and the time for distributing them is during the first few weeks of the new year. You have to grade your gifts according to the person you are giving to, and in some cases these corporate gifts can be pretty flashy or expensive. Also expect that your employees will expect a big chunk of whatever amount of gifts you have allocated to the market as they would want to distribute them to friends and family as a sign of their position. Factor this into your total quantity.

12. During major functions or presentations when you have invited senior officials to attend a conference or the opening of a shop or a factory, you are also expected to make a presentation to this official or group of officials in the form of gifts, which reflects your organization's success and the guests' status.

THE ROLE OF THE FAMILY

It is not possible to overestimate the role of the family in Arab life. To start with, when we talk about family, we go beyond the immediate or the nuclear family to the extended family, and in many countries, the tribe. In some countries, tribes can be as many as 30 or 40 thousand people who are all related by blood. In other countries, there are **tribal confederations** which bring together unrelated tribes under one umbrella and they are effectively locked in a strategic alliance for good or bad.

Whilst tribalism in the grand sense of the word is weakening throughout the Arab world in relation to what it used to be, say, a 100 years ago, it does not mean that they are no longer powerful social institutions. They still play a major part in many functions of the society be it from appointments in public offices to weddings, and from lobbying government agencies to resolving conflicts.

I was once involved in a car accident in Jordan, and the fact that I was a passenger with a cousin did not matter. A girl was hit and although she escaped lightly, the tribal politics of the region where the accident happened meant that both I and the driver had to seek the protection of a nearby tribe for our own security and in order to resolve the issue amicably and away from the complications of a civil courts. It took two days and two nights and endless cups of coffee and numerous visits to the girl's tribe before the issue was resolved. However, had we gone through the civil courts, the issue would not have been resolved for months.

Self-worth or self-realisation, as it is often called in the West, does not come through work, but through the status of our family and what we do for our family. The family also, rightly or wrongly, defines the individual. There are good families, and not so good families, and there are powerful, influential or well-known families, and there are families that are famous for one thing or the other. Arabs are always keen to assess new acquaintances based on their family names. The family unit is also sufficiently strong that it pulls together during crises. Members of the same family will help each other find jobs or assist financially. Marriages between cousins and distant cousins are still common in many Arab countries, especially in rural societies.

Although the Arab culture is often described as being paternalistic, it could be argued that it is equally maternalistic. Both parents play an important role in the affairs of their children and even their grandchildren. It could be added that in the Arab society, age is important, and it is a sign of wisdom and maturity. To most Arabs, old people's homes are abhorrent, and a sign of Western lack of compassion.

MAKING CONVERSATION

The standard advice that used to be issued to all departing expatriates to the Arab World is that they should always avoid talking about politics, religion and women. Whilst I can fully understand the rationale behind this, I have always maintained that this is mainly valid if the departing expatriate is completely ill-informed about these subjects, or worse still, has very negative views about them. My approach to this issue is different. Try and be the one who asks the questions, show curiosity and willingness to learn, and don't be judgemental, and you can talk about any subject you like. It is also my opinion that if you are going to find a local mentor, and this is crucial, then showing curiosity is the only way you will be able to identify a suitable local mentor. Besides, most Arabs are well informed about the negative stereotypes that Western media tends to propagate about them. They are only too happy to give you their point of view.

There are a number of questions that I am frequently asked under this title. Firstly, what other subjects are acceptable? Whilst it is hard to pin these subjects down, it is possible to say that Arabs are much happier to talk about family matters than most Westerners are. The welfare of children, their education and aspirations is one such topic.

Secondly, I am always asked about sports, and whether Arabs like sports and what in particular? Again, whilst it is difficult to generalize, it is possible to say that Arabs are interested in sports. Football is actually the most popular of them, whilst basketball is particularly popular amongst the younger generation. Thirdly, the weather is not particularly a common topic for conversation, as it is in the UK, since it tends to be fairly consistent.

Fourthly, I am always asked about humour, and whether Arabs have a sense of humour. My advice is to be particularly careful about humour, as it does not translate well, and worse still, it could backfire. There are also taboo subjects that you should avoid in humour (such as religion) so try and feel your way. Furthermore, humour that relies on being self-critical is not commonly appreciated in the Arab world. However, situational or spontaneous humour based on sharp observation is appreciated. The Arab sense of humour also varies across the region. It is my opinion that the Egyptians and Algerians have the most wicked, sarcastic and cynical sense of humour. Very often, it is the kind of humour that plays on adversity and hardship as a way of coping with it.

CONVERSATION TIPS

1. The Arabic language is very colourful and Arabs are very warm people, and this will show in the prolific use of pleasantries and the length of the small talk. You could easily be asked, How are you in five different ways, and phrases to welcome you and make you feel warm are scattered throughout the conversation.

2. Small talk and pleasantries will not be limited to the beginning of business meetings, but are the core subjects that you will be coming back to throughout the meeting. Do not be surprised if your host spends more than 15 minutes at the beginning of the meeting with just small talk, neither should you be surprised if they return to it at the end. Small talk here means anything that is not related to business either directly or indirectly.

3. When making conversation, the Arab culture is very anecdotal and idiomatic. Arabs are very keen on telling stories and exchanging experiences. They will frequently refer to a proverb, an idiom or a line of poetry. When your host starts telling you a story you should listen very carefully rather than switch off wondering what this has to do with your question. You may find that the answer is buried in the story and that it may or may not be to your liking, or there may not even be a straightforward answer. Try to learn to tell stories yourself as they are more personal.

4. The Arab culture is a very personal culture, and Arabs are prone to ask questions that many Westerners may consider as too personal. You do not have to answer those questions, but if you do choose to evade them you must do it with skill and flair so as not to sound rude or reserved. Get involved and above all, remember that they want to know the real person inside you, so be prepared to be open.

5. When talking, always make sure you establish good eye contact with your subject(s), and be sure to moderate your tone (don't shout and don't whisper). The Arabic language is not as flamboyant as the Italian language, but it gets close to it, so do not speak with a monotonous voice and be prepared to use gestures with your hands. Also try to face people by turning your body in their direction rather than just turning your head, and it does not harm to lean forward every time something strikes you as being important or funny.

6. In the Arab culture, silence need not be awkward or negative but rather a sign of deep thinking and contemplation particularly when talking to seniors. However, when amongst friends and good acquaintances be prepared to be interrupted regularly.

7. Interruptions by visitors, phones and the regular appearance of a secretary or a colleague are common and need not be considered as rude, aggressive or disruptive. Sometimes it is a sign of dynamism and it is simply very polychronic. The rules of hospitality and open door policy tend to characterise the Arab style of management in a big way.

8. As in any high context culture, the spoken word is supreme and it is superior to the written word, and must precede it where possible. If you cannot meet face-to-face, try to call by phone rather than send a fax or email. The spoken word is more personal, and you can lose too many meanings when using the written word.

9. As in all high context cultures, listen with your ears, heart and eyes. Watch the body language, observe postures and try to feel the tone and tempo. It is all meaningful.

10. Try to learn some Arabic and don't be shy to use basic phrases throughout the conversation. It will impress your counterpart, show your commitment and lighten the situation.

Experiencing Arabia

SOCIALIZING WITH ARABS

Working in the Arab World brings many challenges and rewards. The most important challenge is to integrate into the local society and to expand one's horizons beyond the expatriate community. I am always baffled when I meet returning expatriates who admit that they didn't make local friends, never attended a local wedding, who are unable to master more than 10 words of Arabic and so on. Personally, I question the extent of their knowledge of the country, its culture, and more importantly their effectiveness in their expatriate posting.

Experiencing the Arab culture is about making an effort by being proactive. In all of this, expatriates will find Arabs are very hospitable, willing to help and in many cases flattered by the expatriate's curiosity and willingness to learn. The most damaging preconception that I have ever come across is that

Arabs don't like to socialize with Westerners. For many people, it provides the perfect pretext not to be proactive. Whatever you do, avoid finding yourself locked in this 'ghetto mentality' of 'them and us'.

Furthermore, it is important not to be inhibited from mixing with Arabs due to lack of knowledge and for fear of making mistakes. People will make allowances, and as they get to know you more and better, they will be more than happy to help out in any way they can. You can always rely on this, without being complacent.

There are always questions that you will need a local friend to answer. Making local friends comes through regular interaction and the building of trust, to the point that people are willing to go out of their way to help you out. Take for example buying a carpet. To start with, your local friend can tell you where is the best place to buy it, especially if you are after a genuine Persian carpet. They can also tell you how much to pay and what not to pay. Going with this information is better than going with a blank mind. Bear in mind that in many countries, many merchants have two or three price structures. One for rich Arabs, one for Westerners and one for everybody else. If you impress your local friend enough, he or she may offer to go with you and show you how local bargaining is done.

ATTENDING WEDDINGS AND FESTIVALS

Typically when an Arab wants to get married and declares an interest in the subject, provided that he has no one in mind, his family and immediate friends will start the search to find a suitable bride. The search can take weeks, months or sometimes years depending on how fussy the man is. The search will try to match the status of the man to that of the woman in terms of family background, education, outlook and wealth. Usually after some weeks of search a shortlist is made where the investigation will dig deeper into the background of potential brides.

The next step is the most controversial. In the more liberal societies, a rendezvous is arranged, sometimes under the patronage of the girl's parents in order for the two of them to see whether there is a chemistry of some sort. In the more conservative societies, the sisters or female cousins of the man will try to bridge the gap between the potential couple-to-be. Once there is agreement and consent the third step is made.

The man visits the family of his chosen bride along with his parents and maybe other members of the family where the proposal is made. More often than not consent is not given immediately but rather the father of the girl will ask for time to think about it and to give the girl the chance to think it over. This time is also invested in further investigating the credentials of the proposer both as an individual and on the basis of his family background.

Once consent is given, a second visit is normally arranged in order to finalize the agreement. In some societies, this second visit is a grand affair where the bridegroom-to-be visits the family of the bride bringing with him many dignitaries and elders from his family. A formal proposal is made once again (which is usually just a formality) and the knot is tied.

There follows an engagement period preceded by a grand party, and depending on the desire of the couple, the marriage takes place a few months after the engagement, or in some cases the engagement could last a lot longer. It is normal in Arabic weddings to offer a dowry, but this is offered by the bridegroom and not by the bride's family as it is in some other cultures. The dowry is a controversial amount, but it could be either a tiny amount not exceeding few dollars, or it could be hundreds of thousands. There is also a penalty clause inserted in all Arabic marriages in the event of a divorce where the husband is obliged to pay a specified amount to his ex-wife. Again this could vary from one family to another.

Arab weddings can sometimes resemble carnivals in terms of atmosphere, music, colours and costumes. In some countries, the ceremonies may last several days, and in the more rural areas everybody gets invited. It is an occasion for the whole tribe or extended family to come together and a time for barriers to be broken. In some places, the equivalent of stag nights and hen nights are arranged for both the bride and the bridegroom where they will invite all their friends and neighbours, but needless to say these nights are a lot more conservative than they tend to be in so many Western countries.

Weddings are occasions where the Arab culture reaches its peak in pleasing all of the senses. For most Westerners, it will be an experience of a lifetime as long as you don't mind the crowds. Indeed, it is unusual to attend a wedding party where there are less than 200 invited on the male side and a similar number on the female side. Do note that in some countries separate parties are held for male and female guests, and it is only amongst the sophisticated set that mixed parties are held. Again, in most cases alcohol will not be served but food of all types will be present in plenty.

When you are invited as a guest, but you are not very familiar with either the bride or bridegroom, you are not expected to bring a gift with you. In fact at many of these parties you are likely to receive a gift yourself which is usually a small porcelain vase or dish filled with sweets. In some countries, the close family of the bride and bridegroom will give them cash at the end of the party.

However, do remember that you are not going to get invited to weddings if you have not made friends and shown enough interest in the culture. When invited to a wedding, do remember that you may choose to take a gift with you, but it is often not compulsory and not expected.

It is also important that you try to join in or attend major festivals and public functions whether they are religious festivals, sports-related or artistic functions. The main two Islamic festivals are those of **Eid Al Fitr** (following Ramadan) and **Eid Al Adha** (following Hajj). During these times Arabs will visit each other and normally each visit will not last more than 30 minutes except amongst close family. Some people will make up to 10 visits per day especially in the remote areas. Christmas and Easter are celebrated by Christian Arabs, although sometimes at different times from Westerners.

In terms of sports, football, basketball and handball, are some of the most popular sports in the region. In terms of Arts, most art exhibitions are by invitation only, and so you would need to ask around.

VISITING THE MAJLIS

If you are in the Arabian Gulf, see you if you can visit a **Majlis** in the company of experienced Arab friends. The first time I went I was stunned by the dignity and simplicity of these gatherings. The Majlis is where pure Bedouin heritage relating to access, hospitality and leadership is at its best. The fact that anyone can visit the home of local Sheikhs or dignitaries to greet them or to petition them (without having to go through intermediaries) is something that Gulf Arabs must be proud of and a tradition that I hope will never die.

The Majlis is ultimately the most basic expression of Arab or Bedouin democracy, or Beducracy as it is sometimes called. In Kuwait the Majlis is also called a **Diwaniya**, and the Kuwaiti democratic mindset and tradition is well known across the Gulf. Outside the Gulf, the Majlis is also known as the **Madeef** or **Madaafeh** as is the case in Iraq and the Levant.

Without stretching the concept too far, the Majlis is a simple but effective institution, and in many countries it is a source of socio-political stability. The fact that people can petition local leaders easily and frequently can add to the State's ability to feel the pulse of its population.

Traditionally the Majlis is a very large hall which if stretched can take up to 100 guests, but typically will take about 50-60 people. At the centre of the Majlis, the Sheikh or the dignitary will sit right in front of you as you walk in. Typically, his sons (or her daughters) will sit immediately around him, as well as the most honoured guests. When you walk in, the first thing you do is greet the host and then you have to shake hands with everyone starting from the right of the host and all the way round. You then find a vacant seat while coffee and sometimes sweets are presented to you. You are not always expected to talk to people sitting next to you unless you know them. It is common that you sit next to people for some time and never exchange a word. If you need to talk to the Sheikh, you have to wait for the right time and you then approach him. Typically the conversation with the host should not last more than a few minutes so as to give time to others. You will notice some people handing the host some papers, and in some cases, some of the senior Sheikhs will have one or two aides who will take notes and to whom the petitioner can refer in the future. Typically, your visit should not last more than 30 minutes, and you may find yourself visiting the Majlis several times before you get an opportunity to talk to your host. Some people will visit the Majlis regularly just to maintain contact with the host and without necessarily having some business to discuss.

GOING ON DESERT OUTINGS

If the Arab culture has a spiritual home, it would be the desert. This is not to say that the desert is the only determining factor of it, but it has had a profound impact in shaping many aspects of the Arab culture. It is often argued that hospitality is the finest expression of the desert mindset, and had it not been for hospitality, the Arab race might have perished in this hostile and harsh environment. Furthermore, there are many rituals and taboos that relate to the desert, its climate and pressures.

For example, many of the rituals pertaining to hygiene, food or drink date back to the desert and shortage of water. Furthermore, Arab architecture is very much influenced by the desert. You will notice for example that a traditional Arab home has high walls and small windows from outside. This was to keep both sun and sand out, whilst air circulation was created in the courtyard or atrium which had a lot of greenery in it. Also, the ritual of burying the dead as soon as possible is something that is largely due to desert conditions, which necessitated immediate burial for hygienic purposes.

Go to the desert, but make sure that you go with experienced people and after taking all the necessary precautions. In my opinion, there is something very calm and very pure about the desert, especially at night, where the open sky and the stars induce an air of spirituality and tranquillity that is hard to experience anywhere else in the world. However, the desert is also a very harsh environment that will test your physical fitness and endurance.

In some countries there are specialized tour operators who will organize such outings, and you may also find there are desert clubs in the country where you live. Wadi bashing is now a big sport in the Gulf if you happen to own a 4-Wheel Drive, but it can be a particularly dangerous sport. Sand-skiing is big in Algeria, whilst hot air balloons are popular in Egypt.

You will be fascinated to note that not all the desert is actually desert. Not only will you be amazed with the beauty of the sand dunes, but also you will find there are beautiful and shady oases everywhere. These can vary in size, but some of them will be the size of small villages and some will have, surprisingly, plenty of water. Every now and then you will also come across beautiful mountains or mountain ranges that will truly captivate you. Some of the most beautiful of these are to be found in Morocco, Jordan, Oman and Saudi Arabia. Make sure that you take with you a good camera and plenty of film.

SAMPLING ARABIC FOOD

Lebanese Food is now world famous and is very diverse and nutritious. It can be very rich in vegetarian dishes and also meat-rich. The typical Lebanese Mezza could extend to as many as 80 dishes and the majority of it consists of salads, pulses, grains and vegetables. If you have not already tried it in your home country, you should certainly try it when you are in the Arab world. There are now plenty of books in Western libraries and bookshops about Arabic or Middle Eastern foods, and fortunately, you can now find many of the ingredients in large Western supermarkets or health shops.

Unlike Indian food, and with few exceptions, Arabic food need not be hot or spicy but rather moderate in both. Curry powders for example are rarely used but other spices such as cinnamon, cumin, nutmeg, saffron, turmeric and cardamom are used. Other common ingredients include dried lime, cherries in some parts, and raisins and apricots in other parts. Arabs can also be very keen on herbs such as parsley, coriander, mint, tarragon, rosemary, thyme and sage. There are actually many similarities between Arabic food and Mediterranean dishes. It is a good idea to wander to the spice markets of the Arab world where you will certainly come across spices that you have never seen in your life. These spices tend to be on the whole a lot fresher than in Europe and they are definitely cheaper.

Whilst most Westerners are used to Lebanese food, there is more to Arabic food than Lebanese food, and there is more to Lebanese food than restaurant food. The Arabic kitchen is very diverse and there are many dishes that are best eaten at home. Within the Arabic world there are a number of established cuisines or kitchens. The Gulf kitchen is most influenced by the Indian and Persian kitchens simultaneously, and the cuisine has many vegetable dishes which are healthy. Gulf Arabs also tend to eat a lot of fish and the local varieties are very impressive to any fish lover. One very famous Gulf dish is called **Harees** and it is typically made from camel meat which is cooked with pulses until very tender. **Makboos** or **Kabseh** is yet another famous Gulf dish, along with their local version of the Indian **Biryani**. All are very delicious, and spicy without being hot.

North African food is also famous in many Western countries, especially **Cous Cous**, but it is a dish that varies from one region to another, and sometimes, there are family recipes. My experience is that if you have not eaten cous cous at someone's home, then you have not really eaten cous cous – so start making friends. The cous cous is sometimes accompanied by a chili sauce which is nice in small proportions, but beware – it is extra hot.

The most varied and richest Arabic cuisine is in the Fertile Crescent, and for most Westerners, the Lebanese food is perhaps the one they are most used to. Whilst it is not very different from other dishes in the Fertile Crescent, there are many other variations you ought to try at home.

The Palestinian dish of **Musakhan** is a delight, especially if you happen to like rich food with lots of onions. In Jordan, the most famous dish is called **Mansaf** but as delicious as it is, it can be very taxing on the stomach. The nearest Western equivalent to it is Beef Stroganoff. As for the Syrian cuisine, there is not enough space in this chapter to talk about it. You need to know that there are two Syrian kitchens: the Damascus one and the Aleppo one. Whilst they have many similarities, there are some subtle differences. The most famous of the Syrian dishes are **Kibbeh** and **Cherry Meat**.

The Iraqi kitchen is also very interesting and it is influenced by Persian, Turkish and to a lesser extent Indian kitchens. The most famous Iraqi dish is the fish **Masgoof** which is a kind of plaice that is barbecued inside palm leaves. It has a flavour that is unmatched. Another famous dish is the **Dolma** which is stuffed cabbage leaves, onions and aubergines cooked in tomato sauce.

Arabic sweets are really sweet, but it is rare for Westerners not to like them. To my taste the three most important makers of these sweets are the Syrians, Palestinians and Moroccans. There are literally hundreds of varieties; some are made with cheese, others with semolina, some with nuts and others with sesame, some with dates and others dripping in honey. Marzipan sweets are common in North Africa, whilst in

Egypt there are some really delicious pies. The most famous sweets are the **Baklawa** and **Kunafa**. Do try them, and you will be hooked.

In the main, most Arabs will have their main meal during the day at around 2.00 pm, after which they will go for their siesta. Lunch in this respect is a short affair unless one is entertaining a friend in a restaurant, but even then, it will rarely exceed one hour. Both breakfast and dinner are light meals where cheese, eggs and jams are the most common ingredients.

Invite Arab colleagues to your home and you can be sure that you will be invited back. If there are certain types of food that you can't or shouldn't eat, do tell your hosts in advance and you will not be giving offence. When you invite Arab friends and colleagues to your home, make sure that you serve them something that is from your own culture. However, whatever you do, avoid including ingredients such as pork or alcohol.

SHOPPING AND BARGAINING

If you ever find yourself in Syria, Morocco, Egypt, Oman or Yemen you will come across markets or **Souks** that are hundreds of years old. There you will find the rug dealer next to the silversmith, and the spice trader next to the sweet maker. The experience will be enriching. In some of these cities you will also find separate markets for every trade: one for cookware and one for carpets, one for jewellery and one for spices, one for vegetables and one for meat, one for fish and one for textiles. Nowadays you will find modern equivalents for computers and mobile phones. On the whole, when you are offered such a choice, it is cheaper to go to these specialized markets rather than the mixed ones.

When you are at the Souk learn to bargain and don't be inhibited about bargaining ranges, as you will learn quickly. Go with friends initially and don't buy major things until you are sure about your bargaining skills. However, you must know that there is more to bargaining than offering 40 percent of the asking price. Remember that the customer is king, and you can always come back another time if the price does not suit. Always try to present yourself as an **opportunistic buyer** not a **functional buyer**. Your attitude should be *if the price is good, I will buy; otherwise, I can and will wait.*

However, do remember that there are acceptable or normal bargaining ranges for every type of goods. For example, the highest bargaining range is in textiles and carpets, whilst for jewellery and, for example meat, it is fairly restricted. Equally, many Western or modern style shops may be fairly rigid on prices, unless you are buying several items. Needless to say, modern supermarkets will only offer fixed prices. When you are bargaining make sure that you take your time and whilst you need to show the seller that you are serious, never show them that you are too keen. If you are buying something that is expensive, be prepared to go back several times and try to tell the salesperson that you are not a tourist and you will come back if you get a good price.

More often than not, you will find a much larger range of goods in the local Souks than in supermarkets, and you can be sure it is cheaper. Many of these Souks can be in the town centre, but more are springing up in the outskirts. Ask your local friends for their advice.

If you are going to be hunting for local ornaments or antiques then take your time and ask for advice. Unfortunately there are many badly manufactured imitations which are made in China rather than by a Bedouin in the Sinai desert or a Yemeni villager. You may have to travel outside the capital city into remote villages to find the genuine article, and that is where it can be fun.

GETTING OUT AND ABOUT

There are a lot of outdoor activities that you can do in the Arab world although much depends on the time of the day and how much you like or dislike the sun. One of the most popular activities or experiences that attracts Westerners in big numbers is camel racing which is popular in most of the Arab Gulf states, especially during the winter and spring months. The events can take days, and it is thoroughly entertaining once you get used to the idea, although, as disappointing as it may be to some people, there are no bets. Horse racing is also popular in some Arab countries, and in most cases, you do not have too pay to attend.

Sports in general is very popular, and as in the case of racing, the season really starts in the winter and spring months. The most popular sport is football, and depending on where you are, there are some very good teams. Also in some countries, supporters tend to take their teams very seriously. Interestingly, the sport is gradually acquiring an international flavour with some teams signing up international players. Basketball is popular amongst the younger generation, particularly those who have graduated from the United States. Other sports tend to vary in popularity, such as handball, tennis, cricket and to a much lesser extent rugby. Boat racing and boats in general are very popular throughout the region but specifically in the Arab Gulf states. Both Dubai and Qatar host a number of international events every year. Fishing of all types is also a prime activity and one that is rewarding given the abundance of fish, especially in the Arabian Gulf and some parts of the Mediterranean. More recently, golf has become a very popular sport. Most golf clubs tend to rely entirely on Western expatriates and tourists as the sport is not popular with Arabs.

Cultural events are what most Westerners miss most when they are in the Arab Gulf states. The number of Western plays and musicals is very limited and they tend to be performed by visiting groups and so they don't run very long. However, most international hotels try to compensate for that by constantly inviting international bands, and in some countries, you can go and listen to a live band literally every day of the year.

Depending on the size of the expatriate community you may find that there is a drama society which you can join. The same applies for local musicals. If you are the active type and you like to keep busy, you will find societies galore from basket weaving to snorkeling. Indeed, the common impression of expatriate life throughout the Arab world is 'work hard, play hard'.

LIVING CONDITIONS

It is very difficult to generalize about living conditions throughout the Arab world as they do vary considerably, and they depend on many factors such as the per capita income in any one country, degree of education and level of development or modernization. Living conditions can also vary within the same country according to area, whether one is talking about major cities or rural areas. However, it is possible to generalize that in capital cities and large towns, living conditions, at least from the expatriate perspective, are comparable to what you may find in Europe and North America.

On the whole, and due to an increasing presence of multinationals in the Arab world, you will find that there are now many housing schemes or complexes that are purpose built to meet the expectations of most Westerners. Needless to say that they tend to be located near schools and major facilities, but they can be relatively expensive.

However, there are many places such as Damascus, Amman, Beirut, Cairo and Casablanca where you can experience the local culture at its best. You can rent out old houses in the heart of these old cities for a relatively much smaller sum than modern apartments and enjoy both character and space, but you may struggle with things such as plumbing or water supply. In most of these cities and many others, you will find that Arab neighbours will be more than welcoming, provided that you don't have late parties every night.

As far as health and hygiene are concerned, a degree of diversity does exist; however, you can rest assured that there are many private clinics that you can register with, and most local hospitals are well equipped to handle emergencies and straightforward operations. Within the region as a whole, there are a number of highly advanced health and referral centres such as in Jordan, Saudi Arabia, Egypt and Morocco. Nevertheless, for complex health issues, most patients continue to be referred to the West, particularly to the United Kingdom.

Schooling for Western children is on the whole well established in most Arabic capitals and especially for children up to the age of 15, beyond which children may have to return home. International style American schools will be found in almost all Arab capitals and the same also applies to English schools. The choice becomes slightly limited for French schools and more so for German schools and other nationalities.

Islam: a Way of Life

ISLAM IN THE WORLD

Islam is the religion of approximately 1.2 billion people around the world, and represents nearly one fifth of the world population. It is believed that it continues to be the world's fastest expanding religion.

Although Arabia is the spiritual home of Islam, and the Arabic language is the language of its Holy Book (the Koran), the majority of Muslims live outside the Arab world. Indeed, the largest Islamic nations are Indonesia and Pakistan.

Throughout its history, Islam has been the religion of tolerance and the fact that there continues to be many non-Muslims living throughout Arabia is a testimony to its tolerance. Indeed, at the height of Islamic civilization during the reign of Abbasids in Baghdad and the Umayyads in Andalusia, many of its scientists, philosophers and figures were non-Muslims. Equally, the world of Islam was enriched by its non-discriminatory teachings, which also meant that scientists and scholars of all races and colours contributed to this civilization.

Examples of Islamic history, arts and literature are spread all around the world, from the Grand Mosque in Cordoba to the Dome of the Rock in Jerusalem, and from the Umayyad Mosque in Damascus to the Taj Mahal in India. It is said that Europe's philosophers, scientists and doctors continued to rely on books produced by Muslims until the end of the 18th century. The Western library is abundant with many new books on the subject, and it would be a great shame to visit the Arab world without reading at least one of these books.

Nonetheless, whilst many writers both in the Arab world and in the West talk about the Islamic **Umma** (nation) in a sweeping manner, the world of Islam is a diverse one given its geographic spread and the degree of tolerance that allows several interpretations to exist under the same umbrella of Islam. Thus there is a degree of diversity that exists in how Islam is interpreted and practised that varies from one nation to another. This diversity although very interesting is outside the scope of this book and the book will limit itself to the basic principles that underpin Islam the world over.

ISLAM TODAY

The position and perception of Islam today and around the world has witnessed many changes since the attacks on the World Trade Center on 11th September 2001. Interest in Islam has been heightened and there is now a whole stream of books trying to explain what happened in the light of various understandings of Islam.

The events of 11th September shocked the Arab and Islamic worlds as they had shocked everyone else, and the Arab world is still trying to deal with them on two scores. Internally, many questions have been asked about how a small group of people managed to do such damage in such a short space of time and what purpose did these events serve? Externally, the Arab world is having to deal with the consequences of the event in that international pressure on so many Arabic governments is reaching unprecedented levels and is threatening regimes, civil liberties and stability.

Needless to say that within Islamic teachings, the events of 11th September are barbaric events of great magnitude and they are thus to be condemned without any reservation. There is nothing in Islam that permits or condones the killing of one innocent civilian, never mind thousands. I am not aware of one single reputable Islamic scholar who has done anything but condemn the killing of all those innocent people without reservation. Islam would not have lasted for 14 centuries, nor would Christians living amongst Muslims have lasted that long had Islam included a doctrine that allows the open and indiscriminate killing of non-Muslims.

As in any religion, and as previously pointed out, Islam is a diverse religion that allows for several interpretations, and it has its fair share of extremism, as have most religions and ideologies. Suffice it to say that this book will try to present Islam as it is understood by the vast majority of people *not* as interpreted by an infinitely small group of extremists and disenchanted radicals.

However, notwithstanding the above, and whilst Western perceptions of Islam have been shaped by recent events, the inescapable reality is that Islamophobia has been dominant in the West for some time. This Islamophobia does not help, especially when people are willing to talk about Islamic terrorism but not Catholic or Orthodox terrorism or any other types of terrorism they may wish to brand. Many Muslims feel that they were being victimized before the 11th of September, and, since then this victimization has intensified in both magnitude and scope.

The reality is that there is a need for dialogue. This need can never be addressed through sensational articles in the press or elitist conferences, but rather through an attempt to address the ordinary man in the street in a sensitive and conciliatory manner. Indeed, it has been my experience after 16 years of cross-cultural training that most Westerners will willingly change their views on Islam based on some basic understanding of Islamic principles, particularly the unique links between Islam, Christianity and Judaism.

Within the world of Islam, and in view of recent events and current affairs pertaining to the Arab–Israeli conflict, it is relevant to declare that virtually every religion has its symbols, heroes and rituals. In today's Islam, Jerusalem and specifically **Al-Haram Al-Sharif** with its two mosques is a very important and vibrant symbol of Islam. The religious and symbolic attributes and connotations of Jerusalem are too many to list here. Suffice it to say that it is hard to believe that there could be peace in the Holy Land as long as Jerusalem remains out of reach for Muslims in general, and Palestinians in particular. Indeed, the Arab–Israeli conflict is seen by many Arabs as being the root of all the problems and instabilities throughout the region, and again it is hard to envisage a stable and prosperous Middle East without a lasting and a just, comprehensive peace deal between the Arabs ad Israelis.

As for Islamic heroes, there are many, and you will certainly feel their presence in names of clinics, streets, and schools. These heroes range from scientists such as Aviross and Avecine to military leaders such as Saladin and Tarek Bin Zeyad. Indeed, the Arab sense of history, and its meaning is immense, and this will frequently come up in conversation and discussion.

As for rituals, Islam is actually not as ritualistic as many other religions in both the East and the West. However, there are the five pillars of Islam, three of which will be apparent to any visitor to the region. The first pillar of Islam is the **Shahada** or attestation of faith, which Muslims will repeat many times during prayers. The second pillar is the **Salaat** or prayers, which are performed five times every day. The third pillar is **Zakaat**, which represents the annual alms Muslims will pay to the poor and needy. The fourth pillar is **Sawm** or the fasting of the month of Ramadan where Muslims will refrain from eating or drinking from dawn to dusk for a whole lunar month. Finally, there is **Hajj**, which is pilgrimage to Mekkah at least once in a lifetime. More about Salaat, Sawm and Hajj later.

THE MEANING OF ISLAM

Does Islam mean submission? Yes it is does to the extent that Muslims must put their faith in God but without being complacent. Submission to God means to believe in the one true God, the Creator of all things great and small, and who is Merciful and Compassionate and to Whom Muslims must submit themselves.

In submitting themselves to God only, Muslims must learn to free themselves from all tyrannies of life, whether these tyrannies are to other human beings or whether they are driven by greed, fear, hatred or lust. Submission to God is by no means blind fatalism but an active endeavour to watch and fear God in everything a Muslim does or thinks in relation to themselves and others while at the same time sparing no effort in bettering themselves through lawful, legitimate and virtuous means.

Submission means that Muslims should obey God in whatever they do, and in whatever walk of life they find themselves. In this respect, the concept of Jihad is important in Islam. The root of the word Jihad is J.H.D., meaning to make an effort, to persevere, endeavour and persist, all indicating that Muslims must make the effort and persevere to rid themselves of sin and follow the straight path that leads to virtue and salvation.

The first principle underpinning Jihad in Islam is the duty of every Muslim to better themselves by resisting temptations that are harmful to the individual or society. Jihad in this context is to persevere in the service of God and for the goodness of society as a whole. The second principle of Jihad is to speak one's mind against injustices, and even in front of power. It is what is referred to as 'freedom of speech' to put it in a Western context. Muslims have a duty not to accept injustices but to speak out and not to follow double standards between belief and practice.

The third principle of Jihad pertains to a basic human need to defend themselves, their families, their faith and countries and not to be the aggressors. It is the duty of a Muslim if they find themselves in a conflict to choose peace should the other party choose peace also, and war is perceived as being evil rather than good.

Against the above, it is always a source of annoyance when Jihad is commonly portrayed in Western media as a war cry rather than an exercise in self-discipline.

THE ONENESS OF GOD

In the Name of God, Compassionate, the Merciful

Say: 'God is One, the Eternal God. He begot none, nor was He begotten. None is equal to Him.'

The Koran: chapter 112

Belief in one God, Allah, is the cornerstone of Islam. The **Shahada** (attestation of faith) that 'There is no God but Allah, and Mohamed is his Messenger' is the first pillar of Islam, and the only thing that a non-Muslim has to say to convert to Islam.

The belief in one God makes Muslims monotheists, just like Christians and Jews, and indeed, the whole Islamic faith is based on the belief that Abraham is the founder of Monotheism. It is a duty of all Muslims to revere all biblical prophets and not to distinguish between them. Muslims must also believe in angels and the day of judgement, as will be discussed later.

The belief in one God is in complete contradiction to the Holy Trinity as it is in Christianity, and it is a rejection of idolatory of any type or form. Muslims must worship God directly and not via intermediaries of any type, whether they are idols, icons or saints. Muslims believe that Christ was also a prophet like all other prophets and that Mary is not the mother of God but another human being. Nonetheless, Mary is also highly revered by Muslims as she is held as being the symbol of motherhood, virtue and perseverance of faith.

Another departure from Christianity relates to the crucifixion, where Muslims do not believe that Christ was crucified but rather someone who looked like him. Thus Muslims believe that God intervened to save Christ who ascended to Heaven. In this context, the second coming of Christ is also central to the Islamic faith and in ways that are similar to the Christian faith.

Muslims believe that the Koran is the final, unchanging word of God, which follows on from the Torah and the Gospels, which are important too, being God's revealed words. It is the duty of Muslims to read the Koran regularly and learn by heart as many chapters or **Suras** as they can. Throughout the Islamic world, there are Koranic schools that teach the Koran to children as young as six years old.

MOHAMMED (PBUH): SEAL OF THE PROPHETS

The Prophet of Islam, Mohammed Ibn Abdullah (Peace Be Upon Him), was born in Mekkah in 570 AD into the house of Hashem, part of the tribe of Quraysh. Both his parents died before he reached the age of six, and he grew up in his uncle's house – Abu Talib. At the time the prophet Mohammed was born, the tribe of Quraysh had established itself as the most dominant and noble tribe of Arabia. It is interesting that the position of Quraysh did actually hinder Mohammed's call to Islam in the beginning, and influenced many of the developments that followed Mohammed's death in both positive and negative spheres.

The Prophet Mohammed grew up in Mekkah, which was in his time the central city of Arabia. To start with, it was the religious centre of Arabia where Arabs assembled all their idols at and around the Ka'abah (a cubicle-like building) and it is the place where they performed their annual pilgrimage. The Ka'abah is believed to have been built by the prophet Abraham and his son Ishmael. Mekkah was also the commercial centre of Arabia where Mekkans, through their geographic position, controlled the trade from the Yemen and Indian Ocean at the one end and Damascus and the Mediterranean at the other. In this environment, Mohammed witnessed a wide cross-cultural and religious mix that also made him aware of the injustices of his prosperous city as well as being critical of the polytheism that prevailed throughout Arabia. Mohammed was also aware of both Christianity and Judaism from his early years due to exposure and commercial dealings.

According to tradition, Mohammed received no formal education and could neither read nor write. Disturbed by the polytheism around him, Mohammed began to frequent the cave of Mount Hira', near Mekkah, for reflection and meditation. It is believed that while visiting the cave in 610 AD, when he was 40, he had a vision of a majestic being, later identified as the angel Gabriel, and heard a voice which commanded him to recite. On asking what to recite, he was told: 'Recite "In the Name of thy Lord who created, created man of a blood-clot".' (The Koran, Chapter 96; verses 1-3).

The Islamic call was initially in secret for the first three years, and it was not until the conversion of a notable from Quraysh that it went public. There followed nine years of hard work and persecution by Mekkans and at the age of 52, the Prophet Mohammed migrated from Mekkah to Madinah where he founded his first city-state. This is known as the **Higrah**, and the Islamic calendar marks this date as the beginning of Islamic history. From Madinah, the Prophet Mohammed set out to propagate his message, and the whole of the Arabian Peninsula was converted to Islam before his death in 632 AD.

THE BELIEF SYSTEM

Within the Koran, there are numerous references to explain Dogma **(Al-Iman)** and Righteousness **(Al-Bir)**. Al-Iman is summarized as the belief in God, His Books, His Angels, His prophets and Day of Judgement. These are contained in verse 177, Chapter 2 of the Koran, as follows:

'Righteousness does not consist in whether you face the East or West, the righteous man is he who believes in God and the Last Day, in the angels and the Book and the prophets; who, though he loves it dearly, gives away his wealth to kinsfolk, to orphans, to the destitute, to the traveller in need and to beggars, and for the redemption of captives; who attends to

his prayers and renders the alms levy; who is true to his
promises and steadfast in trial and adversity and in times of
war. Such are the true believers; such are the God-fearing.'

The constant linkage between belief and deeds is a dominant
theme of the Koran. To this extent, Islam is a way of life
because its belief system is an integral part of God's law or
Shari'a as laid down in the Koran and explained by the
Prophet. Indeed, the verse above is an indication that the
moral code is as integral a part of Islam as are the rituals
associated with the worship of God. The goodness of society
as preached by all prophets is echoed in Islam just as strongly.

FAMILY CODE

The Koran is very precise and expansive on the subject of
family and its importance. There are many verses in the
Koran that urge Muslims to be kind and tender to their
parents, to the point that the belief and worship of God is
intricately linked to attitudes and behaviour towards parents
as verses 23-24 of Chapter 17 command believers to do:

'Your Lord has enjoined you to worship none but Him, and to
show kindness to your parents. If either or both of them attain
old age in your dwelling, show them no sign of impatience,
nor rebuke them; but speak to them kind words. Treat them
with humility and tenderness and say: 'Lord, be merciful on
them. They nursed me when I was an infant.'

The Koran goes on to dedicate many other verses that regulate
the affairs of the family, whether it relates to care and duty

towards relatives, marriage, divorce and inheritance laws. Contrary to popular perceptions, divorce in Islam is highly frowned upon and 'Polygamy' is not easily entered into.

A WAY OF LIFE

Islam is often referred to as a way of life due to the fact that it tackles every aspect of everyday life from worship to honesty, from hygiene to hypocrisy, from money to contracts, and from adultery to trade. The following are two selected extracts from Chapter 17:

'Give to the near of kin their due, and also to the destitute and to the wayfarers. Do not squander your substance wastefully, for the wasteful are Satan's brothers; and Satan is ever ungrateful to his Lord. But if, while waiting for your Lord's bounty, you lack the means to assist them, then at least speak to them kindly. Be neither miserly nor prodigal, for then you should either be reproached or be reduced to penury.'

Verses 26-29, Chapter 17

'Do not interfere with the property of orphans except with the best of motives, until they reach maturity. Keep your promises; you are accountable for all that you promise. Give full measure, when you measure, and weigh with even scales. That is fair, and better in the end. Do not follow what you do not know. Man's eyes, ears, and heart - each of his senses shall be closely questioned. Do not walk proudly on the earth. You cannot cleave the earth, nor can you rival the mountains in stature.'

Verses 35-37, Chapter 17

THE MEANING OF SHARI'A

For Muslims, the Koran is the completion of God's message
to humankind and the culmination of all previous sacred
scriptures. Muslims believe that the revelations contained
within the Koran came – like the Jewish Torah and the
Christian Gospels – from a well-guarded tablet concealed in
heaven. The Koran may not be altered by anyone, and is
written in the Arabic language. Translations are available in
most languages today, but they are simply translations that
are open to interpretation and thus it is possible to update
them or criticise the quality of such translations.

Islamic law (Shari'a) derives primarily from the holy book
(the Koran) and from the traditions of the prophet (Sunna); a
body of literature consisting of the sayings and practices of
Mohammed. In this respect, many aspects of the Prophet's
life have been documented and preserved. The life of the
Prophet is believed to be a true interpretation of the Koran.

Islamic law differs from Western law in that, in principle, it is
immutable. It regulates how Muslims relate to the State and
their fellow citizens and also determines their relationship
with God. The interpretation and application of Shari'a Law
varies from one Islamic country to another. In countries like
Saudi Arabia, Shari'a Law forms the basis of all laws, civil
and commercial. In other countries, Shari'a Law is largely
restricted to the family laws.

PRAYING – SALAH

Muslims are required to perform five prayers facing toward the holy city of Mekkah. The times of these prayers are dawn, noon, afternoon, sunset and evening. These daily rituals are supposed to strengthen the relationship between Muslims and their Creator, to remind Muslims of their duties to God and to keep Muslims on the straight path.

For many Muslims these daily audiences with God are constant reminders of God and affirmations of faith. During the prayers, Muslims will recite various chapters or verses of the Koran varying in length, and it becomes a personal thing how long a prayer takes. For some, it can take few minutes whilst for others it can take fifteen minutes, depending on their stamina and degree of devoutness. All of these prayers can take place at the home, office or in the open air or the mosque. Whilst Islam tries to encourage Muslims to pray in the mosque as much as possible, it is understood that personal circumstances can prevent people from doing so. If a Muslim misses a prayer for one reason or another he can perform it later, preferably on the same day. Muslims will also attend communal prayer at the mosque on Fridays. The Friday prayers are preceded by a sermon which can be about any subject whether religious or topical.

All prayers must be preceded by ablutions (Wudu) to ensure bodily purity. The Wudu is a simple routine that includes washing the face, hands, head and feet as well as cleaning mouth, nose and behind the neck.

In some countries, work may be interrupted to allow time for prayers. For practical reasons, and where it is the only choice, group prayers can be performed outside the mosque, and there are now many work-places that provide special prayer rooms. Devout or practising Muslims will break their meetings or journeys (where possible) in order to pray at the appointed time. There are no rules pertaining to what times of the working day you can visit, but it is possible that your host will break the meeting to pray, and this may last up to 15 minutes. Do not take this personally, or be embarrassed by it. If you feel it necessary, you may schedule your appointments not to coincide with prayer times. These are published in all local newspapers.

Finally, non-Muslims should avoid visiting mosques unless they are explicitly allowed to do so, and in this case, make sure that your dress code is appropriate. Depending on the country your are living in, you will find that whilst some mosques will be open for visitors, other mosques may not. There are countries, however, where a non-Muslim visit to a mosque for touristic reasons is frowned upon.

FASTING DURING RAMADAN

According to Muslim tradition and as mentioned in the Koran, the month of **Ramadan** is the month during which the Prophet received his first revelation. Fasting during the month of Ramadan is obligatory for every capable adult Muslim. It is intended to foster obedience to God, compassion to the poor and needy, symbolize unity among Muslims and it is a time for contemplation and meditation.

During Ramadan, the ninth month of the Islamic year, all adult Muslims in good health, excluding pregnant or menstruating women, will fast from dawn until sunset, for 29 or 30 days, depending on the length of the lunar month. Fasting is to refrain from food or drink (or smoking these days) and it is obligatory for Muslims to watch their deeds and their behaviour towards others more closely in order to promote harmony and peace in society.

During the month of Ramadan, the pace of life changes dramatically. Working hours tend to be shorter, and some organizations will start work earlier in the day as well as finishing earlier than normal. Depending on the time of year during which Ramadan falls, it can be harsh or long in some cases or easy or short in some cases. It is common that the period of fasting lasts between 12 and 14 hours, but in extreme cases it could last 16 hours.

The breaking of the fast is called **Iftar** and it happens at sunset. During Iftar Muslims are supposed to break their fast on a small meal of few dates and soup, and then have a proper meal a couple of hours later. Many Muslims will attend evening prayers after their meal, and these last a couple of hours at the most. Prior to sunrise, Muslims have their second meal to give them sustenance for the next day, and it is usually a light meal followed by copious amounts of liquids.

Planning your trip to fall during the month of Ramadan may not be a good idea, unless you specifically want to be amongst friends and colleagues in this important month. Indeed, the social life is very rich during Ramadan, and gatherings tend to go on until late in the evenings. Most international hotels will hold night entertainments which is a mixture of good food and sweets together with music for those who are inclined to listen to it during the month of Ramadan.

Ramadan ends with **Eid Al-Fitr**, the festival of breaking the fast, which normally lasts for three days. This begins with special prayers at the grand or Eid mosque, and where presents are given, and family and friends are visited. The Eid is a momentous occasion for all Muslims and they will visit each other just like most festivals the world over.

PILGRIMAGE TO MEKKAH – HAJJ

The final pillar of Islam is pilgrimage to the **Ka'abah** in Mekkah. The pilgrimage takes place at the twelfth month of the Islamic year (lunar year). All Muslims, and only Muslims, who are physically and financially capable of performing the Hajj, must do so at least once in a lifetime.

On visiting Mekkah, Muslims will repent their sins and ask for forgiveness. The pilgrimage also symbolizes the unity of Islam and equality between people. Pilgrims will wear simple white clothing, and will discard all their riches and appearances in the presence of God. Between 2 and 3 million Muslims from around the world and from all walks of life flock to Mekkah to perform Hajj every year.

At the end of the Hajj period, Muslims will offer a sacrifice to God, which has its roots in Abraham's sacrifice. According to Islamic beliefs, it is Ishmael not Isaac who was spared through the divine intervention, Ishmael being the grandfather of the Arabs. Indeed, the grand mosque in Mekkah contains the Ka'abah (cubicle-like building), which Muslims attribute to Abraham and Ishmael. The Hajj ends with the **Grand Eid** (Eid Al Adha), and the celebration lasts for four days. As in the previous Eid, Muslims will start the first day with a prayer, and will visit one another. Both Eids are also good occasions for Muslims and non-Muslims to visit family, friends and colleagues.

USEFUL TIPS

1. **Dress code.** Keep it modest at all times, for both men and women. Use common sense and observation in determining what is appropriate in the country you are visiting. The dress code for children tends to be more liberal. Dress also tends to vary across each country with it being most liberal in capital or main cities.

2. **Segregation of sexes.** This can be an issue in some countries or within certain organizations, shops or amenities. Be prepared and adhere to rules at all times. Some shops will restrict entrance to some departments to ladies only.

3. **Privacy.** It's up to you what you get up to in private, but keep it that way. Don't try to impose your values or personal habits on the host society, try to blend in rather than stand out. Avoid taking photographs of people, especially women.

4. **Diet.** Don't offer food or drinks containing pork or alcohol. Muslims are not supposed to handle alcohol in any capacity, so be sensitive, and don't display it. Have it hidden in a cabinet if you intend to entertain Muslim colleagues.

5. **Symbols.** Show respect to Islamic symbols whether they are in art, jewellery or artefacts. Try to refrain from displaying non-Islamic symbols in a flagrant or offensive way. Discretion is key to all of this. For example do not put an Islamic painting right next to your drinks cabinet.

6. **Discussions.** Avoid getting drawn into deep discussions about Islam unless you perceive that you are well informed on this subject or religions as a whole. It is not that people are reluctant to discuss Islam, but that you may make big mistakes.

7. **Curiosity.** If you want to know more about Islam, ask sensible questions, and show curiosity. As before, avoid giving misinformed opinions or views that are not based on good, reliable and credible sources. If your extent of knowledge is based on tabloid newspaper articles then it is a lot better to ask the questions rather than make the statements.

8. **Religion.** Don't try to convert Muslims to another religion; it is against the law in most countries. Nevertheless, be sure that if you are religious, people will respect that, irrespective of your religion. Having a moral code of conduct is important.

9. **Fundamentalism.** Avoid the subject if you can, or plead ignorance, as it can be a sore subject. It is considered that the Western media is full of stereotypes on this subject, and the whole issue is grossly exaggerated or misrepresented.

10. **Beliefs.** If you are an atheist or agnostic, keep it to yourself; both concepts remain alien in traditional Islamic societies. Remember, for many Muslims, Islam is a way of life and a system of beliefs. It is difficult for many Muslims to envisage that you could have a moral code whilst at the same time you are an atheist.

11. **Prayers.** Be very aware of prayer times when organising meetings or long functions. You may have to break sessions at the appropriate times or at least be aware that some people may excuse themselves for 15 minutes.

12. **Mosques.** There are some fantastic mosques that you could visit in a many Arab and Islamic countries, but don't assume that this is true for all mosques. Check with colleagues or authorities. Make sure that you are appropriately dressed.

13. **Prayer rooms.** Be aware that many work places will have prayer rooms for employees and workers, so your company may be expected to provide such a room. If you are operating a large international company or a factory with many Muslim employees, it is a very good idea to allocate one room for people to pray in.

14. **Ramadan.** You must not eat, drink or smoke in public during the day throughout the month of Ramadan. Although some of your colleagues may offer you a drink as a courtesy. Also you need to moderate dress code even further during Ramadan.

15. **Festivals.** Do visit friends during the Eid celebrations; it is common, and you will be very welcome. If unsure, find a colleague to accompany you or ask for guidance.

16. **Mohammedans.** Muslims do not like this term, so *never* use it. The term may be out of fashion in the English speaking countries, but not in some parts of Europe.

17. **Inshaalah.** Be sensitive when you use this and similar phrases. Don't respond to it in a sarcastic or humorous way, it may give offence to some colleagues.

18. **Airports.** Expect to be searched thoroughly for prohibited imports, and avoid bringing anything that might give offence or be illegal. It is always a good idea to ask previous expatriates on this subject.

19. **Assumptions.** Don't assume that all Arabs are Muslims, or that they are devout or practising. There are many Christian Arabs especially from the Fertile Crescent, Iraq and Egypt.

20. **Curiosity.** Be sure that if you ask intelligent questions and show curiosity, most of your Muslim colleagues will be more than delighted to answer you or help you out.

Doing Business

THE BUSINESS ENVIRONMENT

To some Westerners, doing business in the Arab world can appear to be chaotic and frustrating. To others, it might appear to be different, but rewarding. These notes aim to explore some of the attitudes and behavioural patterns in the Arab business world, and to demystify them.

Putting it briefly, in the Arab World **business is personal**, in contrast to the business is business attitude common amongst the majority of Western business-people. The Arabs have been traders from ancient times, and to them, business has become a way of life. Furthermore, the strength of tribalism with its emphasis on family solidarity, paternalistic leadership, and relationships all strengthen the link between the business and personal life.

With a better understanding of the Arab approach to business, you will be better equipped to handle meetings, understand tactics, offer compromises, avoid frustrations, see opportunities, avoid conflicts, and correctly interpret subtle signals and gestures. In other words, you will relay the right message and understand the information transmitted to you. Indeed, communication is a two way process: understanding the signals and actions of your counterpart is as important as transmitting them.

Whilst Chapter 3 of this book went into great detail, giving many business tips about dealing with various cultures including the Arab culture, this chapter is more specific to the Arab world. The advice contained in this chapter is designed to heighten your awareness of the Arab business environment and thus prepare you for the differences you are likely to encounter.

The reader would be right to ask 'to what extent is the business environment in the Arab world Westernized?'. The question of Westernization is both complex and controversial. Is it a good thing or a bad thing? For some people, to be described as being Westernized is a form of praise, where for others it is the opposite. Suffice it to say that you will inevitably meet many Arabs who are thoroughly Westernized due to age, education, gender, experience and exposure. However, years of experience have taught me that Westernized Arabs are in the minority. The majority would have acquired many trappings of the Western culture, but deep-down, their mindsets are Arab.

The most outstanding characteristics of the business environment lies in the style of business. Unlike the hectic and stressed business environment most common in the West, the Arab business environment can be described as being relaxed, non-combative, easy-going and certainly non-confrontational. Indeed, these characteristics, whilst being the subject of criticism for many Western visitors to the region, also tend to be what expatriates enjoy most about living in the Arab world.

At the same time, the relaxed environment must not be confused with lack of competition. The opposite is true. It is a highly competitive environment and loyalties tend to shift easily. Businesses will use every tactic to cut prices and will not hesitate to use the competition to get you to cut prices further. It is not unusual to visit one of your longest standing customers in the region and find that your competitor is also waiting to see them. Furthermore, opportunism in terms of one-offs and good deals tend to characterize the operations of many dealers especially in the retail sector. This is despite the fact that long-term relationships are very important considerations for the Arab business environment.

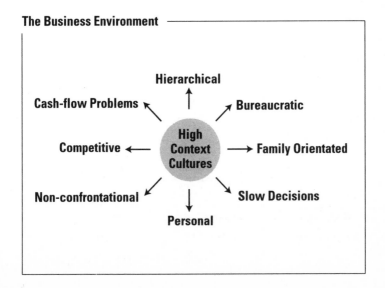

The Business Environment

Hierarchical

Cash-flow Problems

Bureaucratic

Competitive

High Context Cultures

Family Orientated

Non-confrontational

Slow Decisions

Personal

The previous diagram is a brief summary of some of the key features that characterize the Arabian business environment. With the exception of cash flow problems, all of the above-mentioned features will be explored in the next section. The question of cash flow can be attributed to many organizational inefficiencies that exist at macro and micro levels including bureaucracy, slow decisions and lack of forward planning.

BUSINESS IS PERSONAL

The Western approach to doing business is actually unique when it is looked at from outside. Most Westerners have a tendency to divorce and separate their personal lives from business imperatives. The idea that business is personal has more negative connotations than positive ones. It flies in the face of neutrality and can easily lead to bias and favouritism. To solve problems and conflicts, the Western mindset tends to depersonalize them. Business is business in that the Western

Business is Personal

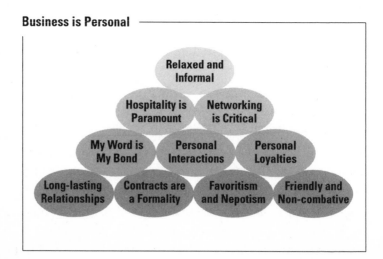

mindset shies away from the concept of allowing personal preferences to influence decisions. The idea that loyalty to the organization must override personal friendships, rules. Rules should never be compromised, and professional standards must be upheld, irrespective of who is involved, whether they are important or not, friends or adversaries, junior or senior.

Whilst these values are admired in the Arab world, Westerners can equally be perceived as being impersonal, cold, direct, lacking compassion and money-oriented. In other words, the concept that business is business can appear to be materialistic. In contrast, the concept of business is personal works on the principle that it is better to conclude a deal on the basis of friendship and trust, rather than on the basis of a contract. Much is invested in cultivating personal and long-term personal relationships that can go beyond rules and personal interests.

THE SPOKEN WORD

There is an old cross-cultural riddle that asks 'who would you rather deal with, someone you can trust, or someone you can sue?' It is a riddle that plays on the importance of trust in business anywhere in the world, whilst at the same time raising a big question mark on how some societies have become more and more litigious. It is perhaps a rule of thumb that the more individualistic a society becomes, the more litigious it is likely to go, and the reverse is true for collective cultures. To this extent, the role of the business contract is often raised in the context of collective cultures. Is it important, or is the personal spoken word more important, and what does a contract mean in collective cultures, and is it different in individual cultures?

As far as the Arab culture is concerned, the bottom line is that the spoken word is far more important than the written contract, and the latter is more of a security or a fall back position. When the relationship has failed, and the use of intermediaries has been exhausted. Contracts are sealed by handshakes first and foremost. Indeed, contracts tend to be perceived more as memorandums of understanding that form the kick-start the relationship rather than totally binding and a point of reference for every incident and dispute. Against this, it is the goodwill that binds both parties that serves as the guide and tool for implementing contracts, and when that goodwill is lost, all kinds of problems can arise.

If we take the three R's model pertaining to contracts, it states that a contract is about stating **Rules**, distributing **Risks** and regulating **Relationships**. All that can be stated here is that in the Arab world, the relationship will underpin the implementation of rules, whereas in the West, the implementation of rules will override relationships.

Notwithstanding the above, it is almost common knowledge that contracts in the Arab world, when viewed outside the relationship context are very harsh. The rules are generally made by the employer and the risks are frequently stacked against the contractor or supplier. This transference of risks, as it exists for example in the contracting industry, is in direct contrast to most contracts in the West. It is said that the local forms of contract as written in most Gulf countries are mutilated versions of the international contracts from which they were derived. Nonetheless, it has to be said that when the relationship between the parties is going well, the contract does not seem to matter a great deal, thus emphasizing the importance of maintaining good relationships as the only safety net available.

THE MEETING

What makes a good meeting? From a Western perspective, there are a number of key factors that will contribute to the success of any meeting. Firstly, the meeting must have a set of objectives that are clear and apparent to all those concerned. Secondly, this agenda must be set against a time frame that is necessary to achieve the set objectives. Thirdly, the objective of any meeting is to discuss issues, raise objections, and make decisions. Fourthly, the meeting must be attended by the decision-maker(s); otherwise it is a waste of time. Fifthly, good time management is a necessity, and as a result, order as intended by the agenda must be followed. Finally, order must mean that where possible, issues are tackled in a structured, linear and eliminative fashion.

Meeting Dynamics

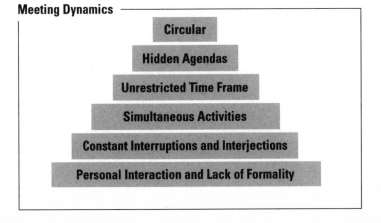

This means that repetitiveness or discursiveness is largely discouraged. Little time is set for personal interaction, and when that happens, it happens at the beginning of the meeting. In a nutshell, the meeting is essentially monochronic. In polychronic cultures, whilst many of the above aspects may be observed, there is a definite difference in how the meeting is run. Most importantly, the polychronic mindset prefers iteration as opposed to elimination; it is more holistic rather than reductionist, and more circular than linear. In plain English, this means that several issues may be raised simultaneously, repetition helps enforce position or clarify points, and circularity allows for flexibility and the ability to leave sticking points for later rounds.

CIRCULAR MEETINGS

The circular agenda means that issues are raised on an *ad hoc* basis rather than linearly, and more importantly, these issues are returned to several times from different angles. This apparent repetitiveness is most frustrating to Westerners who are more linear in their thinking. Once an issue is raised, it is rarely returned to unless it was adjourned. However, the circular agenda has three uses. Firstly, issues are dropped when things get hot or confrontation becomes imminent. This gives each side a chance to rethink and reconsider declared positions. Secondly, the circular agenda enhances understanding, which is important in any cross-cultural dialogue. This is especially true when your counterpart's English is not that great. Thirdly, it is a holistic style of negotiation where no decisions are made until all the issues have been discussed, or every stone has been turned, so to speak. The circular approach can also be described as being both iterative and holistic rather than the linear, eliminative and reductionist style most common in the West.

The Circular Agenda

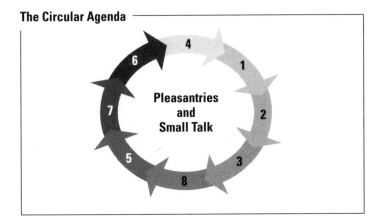

Furthermore, when working with officialdom, it may be the case that your counterpart is not the decision-maker, and thus the negotiation will continue going round in circles, as they cannot commit themselves. They need to refer the matter elsewhere before you get your answers or decisions. However, when you are meeting really senior people who are clearly the decision-makers, the meetings may take on a Western style and be very short. Hence it is important to be concise and to the point, as you may not get a chance to meet them again for some time.

PLEASANTRIES AND SMALL TALK

On first meeting with an Arab businessperson, it would be optimistic, to expect to launch deeply into business. The tendency is to use the first meeting to get to know one another, and subsequently establish a workable personal relationship before the real business starts. By doing so, a kind of safety net is set up to contain future differences and conflicts, which are expected in everyday business. Hence, it is highly advisable to invest time and effort in cultivating a personal relationship. However, this does not mean that business is never mentioned in the first meeting. The discussion may touch on business, but not in any conclusive manner. The issues, offers and ideas will be raised, bounced around and planted in preparation for future meetings.

In the business world, the Arab mind is best described as event driven rather than time-oriented. It means that the dynamics of the meeting are more driven by the circumstances leading to it and underpinning it rather than by the restrictions imposed by business imperatives and time frames. This means that mood, personal chemistry and the circumstances preceding the event will have a major impact on the dynamics of that meeting.

Pleasantries and small talk serve many purposes. To start with, and since business is personal, warmth and trust have to be established to enhance mood and increase the chances of success. Secondly, pleasantries and small talk help to create a bond between their parties and hence their commitment to success. Thirdly, there is a gradual move from personal to business which resembles a build-up that is a form of testing the waters to establish willingness and readiness on both sides. If the mood is good and the willingness is high, then the event is right for going into deep and meaningful business discussions. If the event is deemed to be poor, then going on is pointless, and as the English would say, why 'flog a dead horse?'.

At the beginning of any meeting, much time is spent on pleasantries and small talk. These are not restricted to 'Hello', 'How are you?' and 'Isn't the weather nice today?' They are often genuinely well meaning and extend to all aspects of life (family, hobbies, travelling, current affairs, the economy, etc). These exploratory questions will form the heart of the meeting, and are aimed at creating new relationships or cementing existing ones. To many Westerners, these rituals may appear to be frustrating, uncomfortable and time-consuming. Clearly, this is the wrong way of approaching business in the Arab world.

ORGANIZED CHAOS

Based on years of observation, it is possible to suggest that the Arab manager is a polychronic operator, first and foremost. He or she will possess this innate ability to handle several things simultaneously, just like jugglers in the circus. To the Western mind and ways of doing business, the concept that their host will receive calls, subordinates and guests whilst meeting them is frustrating, disorganized and bordering on the rude. To the Arab, this polychronic behaviour is a good example of normal business practices. My advice is to be patient and not to invest everything in one meeting. Plan for several short meetings, which is what an expatriate friend called 'nibbling'.

What needs to be remembered here is that there are two further factors that add to this state of organized chaos. Firstly, Arab hospitality demands that Arabs cannot leave friends and associates, who are coming to see them with or without appointment, waiting whilst they finish what they are doing. Secondly, lack of delegation and empowerment places the Arab manager under enormous pressure to receive subordinates anytime.

The polychronic manager is someone who treats time as an infinite resource and works on the basis that there is always time to meet people and plenty of time to get things done. Meetings that are going well are easily extended and thus overlaps with other meetings become inevitable. Meetings that are not going well are cut short and rescheduled, thus saving time and sometimes face. There is also the assumption that multi-tasking or doing several things simultaneously is an art and it is efficient, and it is what comes naturally to polychronic managers.

Notwithstanding the above, polychronism need not be perceived as being bad or negative. It has many positive implications, but the most important one is creativity. In the training world, monochronic teams tend to finish the task on time and before their polychronic managers. However, in exercises which require depth rather than organization, and which require creative problem-solving, it is usually polychronic teams that come on top. Polychronic teams are more concerned with the flow of ideas and the spirit of brainstorming than order and neatness. Indeed, I remember a team building exercise which involved both Italians and British managers. The Italian team's comment on the British was that they were great at getting things done but were not all that great at problem-solving. The British comment on the Italians was that they were undisciplined but they were creative. This exercise should serve to highlight that there is a time and place for monochronic behaviour as much as there is a time and place for polychronic behaviour. Successful teams are those who are able to utilize both ends of the spectrum for different purposes.

FLOW AND TEMPO

How Arabs run their meetings is not unique to them. There are certainly many parallels with other Southern Mediterranean and Latin cultures that are on the whole polychronic cultures. The North European and particularly Germanic rush to structure that is also apparent in North America is not necessarily true for the Italians, Spanish and, I dare say, the French. Somebody once called it the 'olive oil' factor.

The similarities between Arabs and say Italians also extend to the concept of silence and interruptions. In most European cultures silence is awkward and interruptions are rude. In Japan and in many Asia Pacific cultures, silence is positive, as a sign of respect or contemplation. However if you take all

Pauses and Interruptions

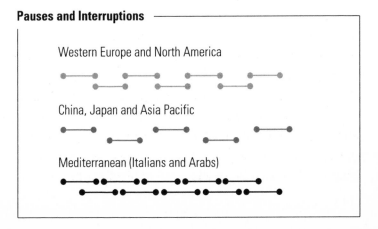

Western Europe and North America

China, Japan and Asia Pacific

Mediterranean (Italians and Arabs)

the Mediterranean cultures and head east through the Arab world, stopping in India, you will find that people will have few inhibitions about interrupting you, and it is possible for several people to speak simultaneously.

The basic advice here is that you should not let interruptions annoy you or make you loose focus, as they do not mean lack of interest or respect. Silence is interpreted as being awkward, although there are times when silence is golden. Try to learn to finish your argument even though others are trying to speak at the same time.

BREAKING BAD NEWS

Many years ago during a conference on culture the discussion moved to the issue of how different cultures break bad news. It was my turn to state the Arab view on it, and I had to admit that whilst I did not have a simple and quick answer, my instinct was that Arabs broke bad news gently, and over a period of time or in stages. The following is how I rationalized my response.

I think that when we are about to break bad news to anyone, there are two dimensions on either side of a continuum. On the one side, there is the task or objective or the truth. On the other side, there is the harmony or need to save face or not hurt feelings. It is the analytical and functional versus the intuitive and personal.

In my personal experience, most Western cultures will tend more towards the analytical and functional, 'get on with it' or 'get it over and done with' or 'get it off your chest' so to speak. Westerners do not like uncertainty and 'time is of the essence'. The Arabs and most collective cultures are more prone to be intuitive and personal where feelings and pacing or timing are very important. However, this is only true in the context of breaking bad news to a friend or someone that is close, and whose feelings are important, and whose face needs to be saved.

Hence, my standard advice on this issue is that if you are about to break bad news then do it gently and in stages. Try to give subtle hints that things may not be going well and you may need to reconsider. Tell them that you are finding it difficult to contain the situation and that there is a distinct possibility that things may not go their way. It is also better to do it in person rather than by a letter, that is if you want the relationship to continue beyond the breaking of the bad news. Remember that these endeavours are supposed to minimize the hurt and save face.

All of the above behavioural aspects, no matter how good intentioned they may be, spell evasiveness to the Western mind. If this is not bad enough, evasiveness can be a lot worse in a minority of cases. This is when your counterpart refuses to meet you on the pretext of being busy or that a decision has not been made. This is when you need your intermediaries most.

PUNCTUALITY

Although Arabs tend to respect and admire good time-keeping, Arabs are not renowned as the world's greatest time-keepers and most punctual of people. There are in fact many Arab proverbs that stipulate punctuality and the importance of time, but they seem to have little impact on reality.

Indeed, lack of punctuality or lax attitudes to time is perhaps the most important level of criticism that Westerners would level against the Arab culture. The reverse is true where one of the most admired characteristics of Westerners in the Arab world is the Westerner's respect for time. It is a riddle that defies any logic but it is certainly true. It does mean that whilst your Arab counterpart is often likely to be late, the worst thing you can do as a Westerner is be late. By being late your are ultimately losing out on one of your most important unique selling points.

The bottom line here is that business meetings could be delayed for some time, particularly if your Arab host has friends or relatives visiting. It is simply against Arab values of hospitality not to welcome them, even though they have arrived without prior appointment.

Hence, patience is a virtue in the Arab World. Indeed, you may often find yourself in a meeting with some of your host's friends, where everybody is expected to join in on the conversation. Having plenty of patience, time and a taste for coffee or tea are about all the preparation one can make in such circumstances.

The subject of punctuality is ultimately related to perceptions of time. This is something that has been studied in depth in the cross-cultural field where it was found that some cultures have long-time orientation whilst others have short-time orientation. For some, the ability to plan and think for a long time in advance is what comes naturally to them whilst for others, they can barely think a year in advance. Whilst the Japanese and Chinese are supposed to think a long time in advance, many African societies are supposed to think in a short-term manner; the now and then.

In the context of the Arab world, it is believed that the Arabs tend more towards the short-term orientation rather than the long-term orientation. It means that plans and proposals should be presented in such a way that captures the short-term potentials rather than the long-term potentials which may not be of great interest. This is not to say that Arabs do not plan for the future, but rather they tend to be more engaged with the tyrannies of the urgent, which is the now and then.

Another dimension of time is how different cultures view the past. For some cultures, the past is more important than both the present and the future, whilst for others, the past is barely important. In the context of the Arab culture, the past is very important, and this is reflected in the very general interest in history, especially the Arab-Islamic golden ages of the Abbasids and Umayyads. In business terms, this interest in the past is manifested through an emphasis on previous relationships, experience, age and track record. A company giving a presentation to a potential client is better off talking about its track record rather than its 25-year vision.

Personal Story: Maybe 1 Month

I was the representative of an international company in the Gulf states during the construction boom of the seventies and early eighties. We sold heavy machinery to the construction sector as well as the oil and transportation sectors. I had several clients throughout the Gulf states, and I made it a habit to keep in touch with them on a regular basis, just to remind them that I was still around.

One of my best but most elusive and shrewd customers was a highly connected contractor who seemed to win contracts based on connections rather than qualification. I made a point of going to see him at least once every two weeks. He was a very entertaining and generous man, and he also seemed to know what was happening in the market and was able to give me numerous leads on many occasions.

I would typically ask him about his next big contract and potential orders to which he would reply that I should learn to be patient in the Gulf, but he would hope to clinch a big deal **maybe** in one month and **maybe** in three months. I would hear this story many times over the coming months without a sign of the big contract, and it became a joke that we both laughed at.

He rang me one day asking me to visit him immediately as he has just signed a big contract. Over coffee and tea we discussed his order of heavy machinery, and he squeezed me on price to my maximum limit. When the conversation drew to an end, he asked me to give a specific date of delivery. Knowing that there were many problems back at the factory in Britain, I tried to fudge the issue by saying it will be maybe 1 month to three months. His immediate response was: 'But you are British, and you don't have maybes'.

British Manager

INSHAALAH

Literally translated, **Inshaalah** means **If God is willing**, and it is the duty of every good Muslim to use such a term when giving promises pertaining to doing something in the future. However, it is most unfortunate that this religious concept is frequently used outside its context, and beyond its original meanings.

Inshaalah can mean many different things. In everyday straightforward business, it is as good as any other promise. On other occasions, it could mean 'I hope so', for example, if you invite someone to visit you when they come to your country. In other situations, if you ask an Arab for a big favour, or for something that he or she is not quite sure about being able to fulfil, an Inshaalah response could mean 'I will try my best', or 'Please give me time and space to think about it', or 'You are my friend, and I do not want to offend you by saying a blank no'. In other words, it can be about face saving, yours and theirs.

Unfortunately, to many Westerners, this is the most frustrating word in the Arab dictionary. This is partly due to the term's frequent use or abuse, and partly due to the fact that many Westerners do not know how to interpret it. The worst thing a Westerner can do is to dismiss the term entirely, carelessly and out of hand. However, they can politely require an explanation in the form of a definite statement.

To the Western mind, Inshaalah spells out uncertainty, and this has to be the most difficult thing for most Westerners. To the Arab mind, uncertainty is a habit and a form of belief.

They will make their plans but at the same time they will accept that such plans may founder at the last minute and for the tiniest of reasons which are outside their control. Fatalism in this context is acceptance with grace.

CONFRONTATION AVOIDANCE

The frequent use of Inshaalah, the need to save face, the importance of pleasantries, the emphasis of small talk and pleasantries, the tendency to follow a circular agenda and the need for patience and good timing are all the signs of a confrontation avoidance culture. The fact of the matter is that Arabs don't like, enjoy or encourage confrontational, combative or explosive meetings. This is an important characteristic of all **collective** cultures where surface harmony can override the task in hand.

Confrontation avoidance can also manifest itself through the use of language whether it is through subtlety, the use of idioms and euphemisms or telling an anecdote. It is said that clever people only need subtle hints. There will be times when you may not get a straightforward 'Yes' or 'No', but where the answer lies in the story or the idiom or proverb. Do listen carefully, and do remember that your Arab colleagues will go a long way in saving your face. This is all part of the **high context** mindset that will go beyond the literal verbal meaning to the implicit meaning. Getting to the truth or rather the bottom line remains your responsibility whereas you have to persist and endeavour to get clarifications on what has been said or implied. Patience, perceptiveness and diplomacy will get you further than being combative.

In the cross-cultural world, it is often said that 'if you go with the flow, you will end up in the gutter'. This will apply to many of your business dealings in the Arab world. You will need to reach a point when you have to ask yourself, 'What aspects am I going to adapt and what other aspects am I going to adopt and what won't I adapt or adopt? Where am I going to draw the line between being global and being local to achieve the optimum glocal level?'

Arabs admire Westerners for their good time keeping and sense of directness (without being rude) which is in a sense an admission of their own failings. The extent to which you are able to maintain a grip on these Western values amongst others will make the difference between being successful and going local. The latter is an indication of going with the flow, which is sometimes the easier option.

DECISION-MAKING

The most basic and apparent manifestation of bureaucracy in the Arab world lies in the decision-making processes, both in the private and public sectors equally. To this extent, there are two incompatible and opposing trends, which are typical of all collective and high power distance societies.

In the main, power and the ability to make decisions is concentrated in the hands of the few who normally sit at the helm of the organization. Delegation and empowerment is limited to those who are considered to be loyal rather than efficient sub-ordinates. This level of centralization is more often than not responsible for immense delays, much to the frustration of clients or citizens.

At the same time, with regards to delays, the role of consultation and the importance of consensus can further block the decision-making process due to the length of time it takes to achieve consensus and is often manifested in committees and sub-committees. The enormity of the number of people that are involved in the decision making process can also add to the confusion. Who is the real decision-maker? Who is blocking the decision? In this respect, the organizational structure or chart can actually be meaningless as it may represent the *apparent* organization not the real organization. On top of all of this, personalities, or more precisely, personality clashes can play a significant role in further delaying or blocking decisions.

The challenge that faces international companies in this context is how to tackle this issue both internally and externally. At the external level, good and reliable information about who are the real decision-makers in the target organization is critical. You are not going to get this type of information from the client, but rather from external sources, be it colleagues or consultants. Once you have identified the decision-makers or power brokers you need to tackle them continuously and simultaneously.

At the internal level, I remember putting this question to a leading Arab entrepreneur. His answer was simple but logical. He always recruits fresh graduates or school leavers so as to avoid people who have picked up bad habits, so to speak.

WAASTA AND FAVOURS

It is most unfortunate that when you mention decision-making processes in the Arab World, you cannot avoid Waasta or Ma'rifa. Waasta is not in principle entirely different from the old boy network in the UK or college fraternities in the US and France. Waasta is summarized by the old universal saying: It is not what you know but who you know. Personal contact, family connections and any other types of affiliations can play a critical role in your success. People can succeed or fail entirely due to their personal connections or lack of them. There is an old Vietnamese saying: For our friends we interpret the law, and for our enemies we apply the law. As an Arab, I wish this was not true anywhere in the Arab world, but unfortunately, there are still too many places where it is the rule rather than the exception.

Whereas in many Western countries, going to the right school or university can have an enormous impact on one's career, in the Arab world belonging to the right family or tribe or coming from the right region or background can make the difference between success and failure. I do not believe that Waasta is unique to the Arab world, but rather it is more apparent and more pervasive than in many other countries that are good at hiding it. This may be a cynical view, but is a conclusion I have reached after years of experience on the international stage.

Looking at Waasta from a completely different perspective, it is possible to say that it emerges as a direct response to bureaucracy in as far as being the only way anything can get done. If you talk to people, they will tell you that they feel bad about Waasta, that they would rather not use it, and they would prefer to see some reform in the government systems. However, Waasta can sometimes be about favours where people will do their best to help you, sometimes irrespective of whether they know you or not. If you happen to be a friend, a friend of a friend or if they happen to like you, respect you or even like the way you talk to them, then you can turn them into allies rather than adversaries. In a nutshell, business is personal.

As collectivists, Arabs cherish warm social interactions above everything else. They do not understand individualism as a social system and find it difficult to understand reclusive or eccentric individuals. Social interaction and the need for conformity come at a price. The giving and receiving of favours is very common amongst friends, to the extent that one uses one's friends to a level that contradicts the meaning of friendship for most Westerners.

EXERCISE – MAKING A PRESENTATION

You have been invited by an important Arab client to give a presentation on your company's range of products or services. You have been given 3 hours, and it was suggested that about 50 people would attend. The presentation will take place in the morning at an international hotel.

As a first step, in your own culture, what will be your most important five considerations?

1.

2.

3.

4.

5.

In the Arab culture, what will be your most important five considerations?

1.

2.

3.

4.

5.

OUR ANSWER

Here are some key suggestions that you may find useful, but the list is by no means exhaustive:

1. Acknowledge patronage and ask if the host wishes to address the audience.
2. Mobilize network and contact invitees (a few days beforehand) personally to ensure a good attendance.
3. Pay compliments if and where possible. Any flattery you use must be genuine.
4. Ensure someone at a senior level is present from your own company, and that they participate.
5. Ensure adequate seating arrangements for the senior attendees.
6. Play up past relationships and experiences and talk about previous achievements.
7. Get a proper brief on who is who, why they are there, and what is their role or position.
8. Hospitality is vital. Organize coffee breaks and consider inviting everyone for lunch.
9. Ensure that there are lots of brochures, promotional material and freebies.
10. An exhibition, a short film or a demonstration (visual aids) always goes down well.
11. Talk about 'realisable' and short- to medium-term projects and products.
12. Presentations must be authoritative and definitive (you are the experts).
13. Questions are more likely to emerge during coffee breaks than during the presentation.
14. You must show that you believe in your product. Do not be too neutral; be sincere.
15. Ensure good eye contact, use personal anecdotes to demonstrate a point – be yourself.

Recommended Reading

Islam and History

Arab Thought in the Liberal Age
Albert Hourani, Cambridge University Press, 1988

A History of the Middle East
Peter Mansfield, Penguin Books, 1992

Islam: The Straight Path
John Esposito, Oxford University Press, 1994
(ISBN: 0-19-507472-6 (pbk))

The Crusades Through Arab Eyes
Amin Maalouf, Alsaqi Books, 1983

Fiction

Samarkand
Amin Maalouf, Abacus, 1995

Leo the African
Amin Maalouf, Abacus, 1995

Miscellaneous

Yamani: The Inside Story
Jeffrey Robinson, Fontana Collins, 1990 (ISBN: 0-00-637408-5)

Tribes with Flags: A Journey Curtailed
Charles Glass, Picador, 1990 (ISBN: 0-330-31930-2)

Management Worldwide
David J. Hickson & Derek S. Pugh, 1995 (ISBN: 0-14-014981-3)

Index